CLINICAL INFERENCE:
HOW TO DRAW
MEANINGFUL CONCLUSIONS
FROM PSYCHOLOGICAL TESTS

CLINICAL INFERENCE:
HOW TO DRAW
MEANINGFUL CONCLUSIONS
FROM PSYCHOLOGICAL TESTS

Audrey Myerson O'Neill

Clinical Psychology Publishing Co., Inc.
4 Conant Square
Brandon, Vermont 05733

Library of Congress Cataloging-in-Publication Data

O'Neill, Audrey Myerson, 1928-
    Clinical inference : how to draw meaningful conclusions from
psychological tests / Audrey Myerson O'Neill.
        p.   cm.
    Includes bibliographical references and index.
    ISBN 0-88422-117-2 (paper) : $24.95
    1. Psychological tests for children--Interpretation.
    2. Psychological tests--Interpretation. 3. Psychodiagnostics.
    I. Title.
    [DNLM: 1. Judgment. 2. Psychological Tests. 3. Psychology,
Clinical--methods.   BF 431 058c]
RJ503.5.053   1992
155.4'0287--dc20   92-52846
                                                    CIP

 4 Conant Square
Brandon, Vermont 05733

Cover design: Michael F. Gauthier

Printed in the United States of America.

Thanks

to

Plymouth State College, University System of New Hampshire,
which for many years has provided me, as faculty family,
with home, community, colleagues, and resources;
and especially to
my husband, Robert E. O'Neill of the Philosophy Department;
present and past members of the Psychology Department;
and the staff of Lamson Library,
especially the Reference and Interlibrary Loan Departments.

CONTENTS

INTRODUCTION

The challenge facing a psychological examiner is to make sense of the information gathered in the examination process. Only meaningful conclusions can serve as a basis for decisions that are realistic, constructive, and just.

This book presents the approach that test interpretation is a task of integrating the information into a cohesive and plausible account. The results should explain the stated presenting problem — and the sometimes unspoken concerns the examiner finds behind the referral — plus any surprise issues that occasionally come to light.

This approach differs in scope and emphasis from the method of test interpretation currently popular. The method currently in vogue depends heavily on differences among partial test scores — subscales, subtests, or factors — almost to the exclusion of other information. These score differences are called *scatter*. Scatter is usually interpreted by either equating a separate ability with each subtest or subtest cluster, or comparing clusters with patterns established empirically for known populations.

Two historical trends have led to the preeminence of scatter analysis in test interpretation. The first is the great importance to the field of psychology over the last 50 years of *quantification*.

When psychology was a relatively new field, it was regarded by people in other fields as less scientific than the older sciences because the subject matter does not lend itself as readily to measurement. The anthem of the detractors of descriptive, or "soft," psychology was, "Whatever exists, exists in some amount [and can be measured]."[1] An irreducible part of the subject of clinical psychology, however, exists in amounts of one, which limits the possibility of total quantification, except by rejecting the nonconforming data as unworthy of consideration. Just as psychology was looked down on by other sciences, clinical psychology was looked down on by other fields of psychology, with experimental psychology considered the model field.

No longer is this the case. By embracing statistics, psychology came of age as a real science and has commanded heightened esteem because of its contribution to human well-being, as well as its intrinsic interest. Clinical psychology has acquired enhanced status within the field of psychology because of the growth of the mental health movement. Psychologists concerned with scientific method now accord explanations about individuals (narrative truth) equal billing with proof about populations (correspondence truth) (Sarbin, 1986). "If you only study things that can be measured, then you are studying the wrong things" (paraphrased).[2] Yet numerical test scores have retained their glamour, their aura of precision.

The other trend contributing to the emphasis on scatter analysis is the sheer acceleration in volume of testing. The mental health movement has contributed to this growth. So has the Individuals with Disabilities Education Act (the 1990 revision of the 1975 Education for All Handicapped Act), which has shifted the burden for the major part of the testing of persons under 18, and in some states 21, to the schools.

The schools were not prepared for this mandate, but it was nevertheless theirs; and, a system of testing has developed in response in which the emphasis is often, although not always, on quantity and economy. There has been increased pressure for school examiners to give more tests and give them faster, and for more people to become examiners. Quality safeguards won by the psychology profession have had little effect on this growing army of examiners, some psychologists and some not. Most examiners are rushed, many harassed, some inadequately prepared, and some caught in conflict between child advocacy and district financial interests.

Scatter analysis fit this need for volume in testing. If test interpretation could be made purely mechanical, then 2-hour workshops would suffice to pass the torch of teaching test interpretation. The evaluation process could be streamlined into the kind of piecemeal, assembly-line operation that is sometimes justified as "multidisciplinary."

Examiners could serve as pairs-of-hands[3] disconnected from the inference process, and diagnosis and decision making could be further removed from those who do the work of testing. The effect is to reduce the role of testing to a trivial clerical job, unworthy of a professional, a poor third to consultation and therapy. (*"I* don't do testing. I'm a *consultant."*)

The Individuals with Disabilities Education Act, however, states that a child must receive an *individual* psychological examination. The mechanical comparison of subscales or subtests with a mean or norm hardly fits that requirement.

The individualized approach to test interpretation is designated by the word *clinical. Clinical* is often misunderstood to mean "intuitive," or "pertaining to pathology," but it really means *applied, individualized.* The clinic is where specialists in the health/helping/education professions apply knowledge about people and their problems to real-life subjects, none of whom is exactly like the textbook model or the experimental population because each is a unique individual.

It is much more difficult to teach clinical inference than scatter analysis. Scatter analysis follows comparatively few, simple rules, whereas individualized test interpretation integrates additional information and draws on background knowledge that may be far from complete at the time testing is first undertaken.

For this reason, clinical inference has been compared to two skills of considerably less intellectual status. One is determining the gender of newborn chicks, a completely subliminal discrimination many people can learn by example without much difficulty. The other is water dowsing, a practice that has both doubters and believers, and is also done without conscious understanding. Dowsing requires no training and can be done by some constant proportion of the population, with no known way of predicting individual success.

Like chicken sexing, clinical inference has been considered teachable only by example rather than by a definable method befitting a science; like water dowsing, it has been considered learnable only by persons with inherent and somewhat suspect powers. However, all practical knowledge is taught by example, learned by practice, and comes more easily to some than to others.

The purpose of this book is to describe the clinical inference process so that people can more easily communicate about it, teach it, and learn it. The book is addressed primarily to practitioners, students, the students' teachers, and anyone interested in the inference process. It assumes some familiarity and experience with testing. The emphasis is on the ordinary practitioner in the ordinary workplace rather than the ideal professional in ideal circumstances. Growing out of the conclusions from this grass-roots approach, however, are recommendations not only for examiners but for those who control them: school and government administrators, and leaders in the profession.[4] In all fields, many problems are caused by separation between those who do the work and those who decide how it is to be done.

Chapter 1 compares different levels of interpretation of the same case. The *level* is the extent to which the examiner has drawn individualized conclusions. In some cases, the individualized interpretation is quite different from the interpretation based on scatter analysis. These cases are like "crucial experiments," which are set up to test two opposed theories by finding an area where their predictions differ, so that only one can be confirmed.

Chapter 2 offers examples of an often-neglected kind of data necessary for individualized interpretation. Chapter 3 attempts to approximate the frequency of cases where individualized interpretation differs from score interpretation, through a study of a moderate number of cases. The first part of Chapter 4 describes the method of reasoning used in individualized interpretation and underlines the similarity between clinical reasoning and reasoning in other fields of knowledge. The second part of Chapter 4 applies this method to case illustrations. Chapter 5 presents more cases, and Chapter 6 discusses the effects of outside constraints on the inference process.

One case appears throughout in *spiral* presentation, a term borrowed from the spiral curriculum which repeats the same content at different grade levels in increasing detail and complexity. The case shown at different levels of interpretation in Chapter 1 also serves as the main example of applied reasoning in Chapter 4.

The tests discussed are taken from school evaluations, without attempting to sample the whole field. The Kaufman Assessment Battery for Children, the Stanford-Binet Intelligence Scale: 4th edition, and the Wechsler Intelligence Scale for Children — Revised (WISC-R) are represented in such a way as to highlight their usefulness. Other tests appear more briefly.

The greatest proportion of examples feature the WISC-R. The reason for this is partly situational and partly rhetorical. It was by far the most popular test in the region where the case illustrations were collected, and in the nation (Goh, Teslow, & Fuller, 1981). It has also proved far more subject to misleading scatter effects than the other tests. Wechsler originally created his test to introduce equal representation of nonverbal ability into intelligence testing. Subtests were chosen on the purely empirical basis of how well they contributed to the whole test, with no intent to exemplify the separate abilities they are often interpreted to represent. Therefore, when used as measures of specific abilities, Wechsler subtests are far more often contaminated with other factors than tests developed more recently around learning models for special education. This is not an indictment of Wechsler's tests but of their improper interpretation. Their very contamination adds richness in opportunities for behavioral observation. All tests are to some extent contaminated.

An ability is an abstraction derived from behavior, something we think we see behind behavior. We presume that the ability corresponds to some basic tangible thing, a neurological structure or operation — perhaps genetically determined, perhaps honed by practice — which will express itself in a variety of behaviors of the same type. But a specific correspondence has not always been demonstrated. Some classifications of abilities that are very helpful to teachers in understanding learning behavior, like the Illinois Test of Psycholinguistic Abilities, do not necessarily correspond to specific structures or operations of the brain. Reasoning from one behavior to another may or may not be valid. The person who shows a high, or low, level of performance at, say, supplying missing details on Wechsler's Picture Completion subtest, may or may not perform to a similar degree at detecting small differences among lowercase letters, fingerprints, the faces of new acquaintances, engine models, or birds in flight. It is the job of the examiner-interpreter to determine which information leads to which conclusions *in the particular case.*

It is hoped that this book, in describing the role of the individual examiner in the evaluation of the individual subject, will help restore some of the esteem and authority earlier associated with testing. For this purpose, a case is appended illustrating the sometimes therapeutic effects of testing. (See Appendix 1.)

Problem solving is hard work, but it can be learned, and it has intrinsic rewards: In learning how to make sense of the multiple, complex data of a psychological examination, one also begins to be able to make sense of the rest of life.

1 LEVELS OF INTERPRETATION

Test reports differ in the amount of interpretation the examiner has done. Some reports give little interpretation beyond test scores, whereas others base conclusions on a complex process of problem solving. This chapter presents three degrees of interpretation, called *levels,* starting with the level giving the least amount of interpretation.

LEVEL 1. THE CONCRETE LEVEL: JASON

Example 1-1 shows a concrete-level test report. The interpretation in Example 1-1 is limited to a list of equivalencies of the subtests and

---

Example 1-1

Name: Jason
Age: 10-8

Test Results:

The Wechsler Intelligence Scale for Children — Revised is a test of general ability. It has two parts, a Verbal Scale and a Performance Scale. The Verbal Scale IQ shows the child's verbal ability, and the Performance Scale IQ shows the child's perceptual-motor ability. The Full Scale IQ shows the child's general ability.

(continued)

Example 1-1 *(continued)*

The Wechsler Intelligence Scale for Children — Revised has twelve subtests, half verbal and half performance. Eleven subtests were given.

On the Information subtest, the examiner asks the child to answer questions from the child's fund of general factual knowledge. On this subtest, Jason obtained a raw score of 15. This is equivalent to a scaled score of 10. A scaled score of 10 is at the 50th percentile rank. Jason is at the 50th percentile rank among children his age. This is in the average range. Jason is in the average range in fund of general factual knowledge. A raw score of 15 has an age-equivalent of 10-10. Jason performed on this test as an average child age 10-10.

On the Similarities subtest, the examiner asks the child to tell how two things are alike. This shows the child's ability in verbal concept formation. On this subtest, Jason obtained a raw score of 11. This is equivalent to a scaled score of 8. A scaled score of 8 is at the 25th percentile rank. Jason is at the 25th percentile rank among children his age. This is in the average range. Jason is in the average range in verbal concept formation. A raw score of 8 has an age-equivalent of 9-2. Jason performed on this subtest as an average child age 9-2.

On the Arithmetic subtest, the examiner asks the child arithmetic problems aloud, and the child solves them mentally. This shows the child's computational skills. On this subtest, Jason obtained a raw score of 11. This is equivalent to a scaled score of 9. A scaled score of 9 is at the 37th percentile rank. Jason is at the 37th percentile rank among children his age. This is in the average range. Jason is in the average range in computational skills. A raw score of 11 has an age-equivalent of 9-6. Jason performed on this subtest as an average child age 9-6.

On the Vocabulary subtest, the examiner pronounces a word, and asks the child to tell the meaning of the word. This shows the child's word knowledge. On this subtest, Jason obtained a raw score of 30. This is equivalent to a scaled score of 9. A scaled score of 9 is at the 37th percentile rank. Jason is at the 37th percentile rank among children his age. This is in the average range. Jason is in the average range in word knowledge. A raw score of 30 has an age-equivalent of 10-6. Jason performed on this subtest as an average child age 10-6.

On the Comprehension subtest, the examiner asks the child common-sense questions. This shows the child's practical knowledge. On this subtest, Jason obtained a raw score of 18. This is equivalent to a scaled score

(continued)

Example 1-1 *(continued)*

of 10. A scaled score of 10 is at the 50th percentile rank. Jason is at the 50th percentile rank among children his age. This is in the average range. Jason is in the average range in practical knowledge. A raw score of 18 has an age-equivalent of 10-10. Jason performed on this subtest as an average child age 10-10.

On the Digit Span subtest, the child is asked to repeat series of digits after the examiner. This shows the child's short-term auditory memory. On this subtest, Jason obtained a raw score of 9. This is equivalent to a scaled score of 7. A scaled score of 7 is at the 16th percentile rank. Jason is at the 16th percentile rank among children his age. This is in the low average range. Jason is in the low average range in short-term auditory memory. A raw score of 9 has an age-equivalent of 7-6. Jason performed on this subtest as an average child age 7-6.

On the Picture Completion subtest, the child is asked to name the parts missing from pictures. This shows the child's visual alertness and long-term visual memory. On this subtest, Jason obtained a raw score of 20. This is equivalent to a scaled score of 12. A scaled score of 12 is at the 75th percentile rank. Jason is at the 75th percentile rank among children his age. This is in the high average range. Jason is in the high average range in visual alertness and long-term visual memory. A raw score of 20 has an age-equivalent of 12-6. Jason performed on this subtest as an average child age 12-6.

On the Picture Arrangement subtest, the child is presented with a scrambled series of pictures, and asked to arrange them in a story sequence. This shows the child's time sequencing and social understanding. On this subtest, Jason obtained a raw score of 31. A raw score of 31 is equivalent to a scaled score of 11. A scaled score of 11 is at the 63rd percentile rank. Jason is at the 63rd percentile rank among children his age. This is in the average range. Jason is in the average range in time sequencing and social understanding. A raw score of 31 has an age-equivalent of 13-10. Jason performed on this subtest as an average child age 13-10.

On the Block Design subtest, the child is asked to arrange patterned blocks to match a design shown. This shows the child's ability in nonverbal concept formation and visual analysis. On this subtest, Jason obtained a raw score of 31. A raw score of 31 is equivalent to a scaled score of 11. A scaled score of 11 is at the 63rd percentile rank. Jason is at the 63rd percentile rank among children his age. This is in the average range. Jason is in the average range in nonverbal concept

(continued)

Example 1-1 *(continued)*

formation and visual analysis. A raw score of 31 has an age-equivalent of 11-6. Jason performed on this subtest as an average child age 11-6.

On the Object Assembly subtest, the child puts together disarranged picture-puzzles. This shows the child's ability in visual synthesis. On this subtest, Jason obtained a raw score of 26. A raw score of 26 is equivalent to a scaled score of 13. A scaled score of 13 is at the 84th percentile rank. Jason is at the 84th percentile rank among children his age. This is in the high average range. Jason is in the high average range in visual synthesis. A raw score of 26 has an age-equivalent of 15-6. Jason performed on this subtest as an average subject age 15-6.

On the Coding subtest, the child must encode symbol substitutions using a pencil. This shows the child's clerical speed and accuracy, and short-term visual memory. On this subtest, Jason obtained a raw score of 38. A raw score of 38 is equivalent to a scaled score of 8. A scaled score of 8 is at the 25th percentile rank. This is in the average range. Jason is in the average range in clerical speed and accuracy, and short-term visual memory.

Jason obtained a Verbal Scale IQ of 95. An IQ of 95 is at the 37th percentile rank. Jason is at the 37th percentile rank among children his age. This is in the average range. Jason is in the average range in verbal ability.

Jason obtained a Performance Scale IQ of 106. An IQ of 106 is at the 66th percentile rank. Jason is at the 66th percentile rank among children his age. This is in the average range. Jason is in the average range in perceptual-motor ability.

Jason obtained a Full Scale IQ of 100. An IQ of 100 is at the 50th percentile rank. Jason is at the 50th percentile rank among children his age. This is in the average range. Jason is in the average range in general ability.

subscales. The subtest equivalencies are the product of armchair *task analysis,* not empirical research. Although on the whole they make very good sense, they are assumptions.

In the coin of the realm, Example 1-1, showing the Level 1 test report, has strengths and weaknesses, good news and bad news. The good news is that everything it says is true. Its failings are best shown by an equivalent alternative, Example 1-2. As the optometrist asks,

showing two different views of the same material, which is clearer,
Example 1-1 or Example 1-2?

Example 1-2

Jason, 10-8

Wechsler Intelligence Scale for Children — Revised

Verbal Tests		Performance Tests	
Information	10	Picture Completion	12
Similarities	8	Picture Arrangement	11
Arithmetic	9	Block Design	11
Vocabulary	9	Object Assembly	13
Comprehension	10	Coding	8
(Digit Span)	(7)		

Verbal Scale IQ	95	Performance Scale IQ	106
	Full Scale IQ	100	

For those who prefer to include percentile ranks (PR)[1] and age
equivalents (AE), as well as scaled scores (SS), there is Example 1-3.

Example 1-3

Jason, 10-8

Wechsler Intelligence Scale for Children — Revised

Verbal Tests	SS	PR	AE
Information	10	50	10-10
Similarities	8	25	9- 2
Arithmetic	9	37	9- 6
Vocabulary	9	37	10- 6
Comprehension	10	50	10-10
(Digit Span)	(7)	16	7- 6
Performance Tests			
Picture Completion	12	75	12- 6
Picture Arrangement	11	63	13-10
Block Design	11	63	11- 6
Object Assembly	13	84	15- 6
Coding	8	25	9-10
Verbal Scale IQ	95	37	10- 2
Performance Scale IQ	106	66	12- 7
Full Scale IQ	100	50	10- 8

Examples 1-2 and 1-3 are clearer than Example 1-1 because they do not bury the information in unnecessary sentences. The description of the test and subtests adds nothing. A written report is not the place to educate people about the WISC-R. Those unfamiliar with the test will not gain real understanding from a thumbnail description, and those familiar do not need it. Brief descriptions risk imparting a superficial familiarity with the test that readers easily mistake for working knowledge. Personal explanations of tests do not have this effect because they are tailored to individual cases rather than generalized, and they lack the catchiness of the capsule phrases.

Examples 1-2 and 1-3 are also preferable for economy — of the reader's time if not the writer's and typist's, should the document be duplicated with blanks to be filled in.

Another reason for preferring Examples 1-2 and 1-3 is the principle of *simplicity*, which in science is called Occam's Razor. Some students learn the opposite principle in courses where a long paper is more likely to be rewarded with an A than a short one with the same idea content. The principle of simplicity, nevertheless, has considerable influence both in science and in the culture as a whole. Some of its names and cultural expressions are listed in Table 1. Simplicity, however, is not to be confused with simple-mindedness. The criterion for including material is not easy reading but relevance.

The hallmark of Level 1 interpretation is that *it does not draw conclusions beyond scores*. Other characteristics of Level 1 are listed in Table 2.

With its emphasis on subtest scores, Level 1 interpretation treats subtests as if they represent distinct abilities and translates them into something more real and tangible than they are. (See Figure 1.)

Occam's Razor

William of Occam (1285–1349), a medieval philosopher, founded a principle (the Law of Parsimony) that is still basic to contemporary thought. It might be stated: *Do not introduce more factors into your reasoning than necessary*. This principle has been called Occam's Razor because it cuts or shaves off unnecessary material.

How many factors are necessary, however, depends on the goal of the reasoning and the state of knowledge in the field.

Table 1
Names and Expressions of the Principle of Simplicity

Occam's Razor	Contemporary furniture and
Law of Parsimony	architecture
Thoreau's *Walden*	The Uncluttered Look in fashion and
Less is More	interior decoration
Small is Beautiful	Minimalist art, literature, and
Enough is as good as a feast	design
Streamlined automobiles and	K.I.S.S. (Keep it simple,
appliances	Sweetheart)

Table 2
Characteristics of Level 1

Concrete	Descriptive
Test-centered	Enumerative
Does not draw conclusions	Laundry list

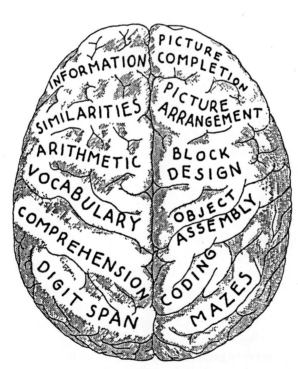

Figure 1. A psychometrist's misconception of the human brain.

LEVEL 2. THE MECHANICAL LEVEL: JASON REVISITED

The mechanical level of interpretation is concerned as much, or more, with the differences among the subtests and subscales of a test, as with the scores themselves. This calls for a standard for judging whether differences among scores are large enough to matter. More recent tests have this information easily accessible in the manual. The WISC-R does not. There are statistical formulas for making this determination, involving varying amounts of table searching and calculation. The more accurate the results promised, the more cumbersome the formula, to the point that anyone with the ability and inclination to do the computation would probably not be examining children for a living. This is another of the many pressures that make practitioners feel like losers in the game of work. (See Chapter 6.)

Fortunately, Alan Kaufman (1979, pp. 24;[2] 54) has rescued practitioners from this quandary by generalizing and simplifying considerable information into two *practitioners' rules* that allow examiners to fairly breeze through mechanical interpretation of the WISC-R.

Knowledge, however, is never complete. Even as these words were being written, the sands of knowledge were shifting once more, and new knowledge was changing the rules (A. S. Kaufman, personal communication, March 21, 1990).

Remember Jason? Jason's examination date is October, 1988, before the rule change trickled down. The theoretical journal article (Silverstein, 1982) had already appeared. But practitioners do not live by theoretical articles. They live by textbooks and workshops by experts' experts—often theoreticians in their own right—who translate knowledge and pass it along.

When Jason was tested, the practioners' rule found his Coding score significantly low. The current revision says it is not.

The only feasible response to scientific progress—for such this is—that changes the rules, is to decide how much difference it really makes; accept the truth in past findings while remembering the difference; and also remember that the community accepted them at the time. (See *Unplanned Obsolescence,* Chapter 4, p. 109.)

The change of rules makes relatively little difference in this case. Therefore, this discussion will allow the interpretation of Jason's scores, by the practice of their time, to stand, and will reserve the sobering double vision of hindsight. The price of scientific progress is having to run as fast as possible in order to stay in the same place, like trying to walk up a DOWN escalator.

Even by 1988 rules, there is a problem. By definition, practitioners'

Kaufman's Practitioners' Rules
for Interpreting WISC-R Scores

1979, Intelligent Testing with the WISC-R:[a]

On interpreting Verbal–Performance IQ Differences:

> The size of V–P differences required for statistical significance is . . . 12 points ($p < 0.05$), and 15 points ($p < 0.01$). . . . For V–P comparisons, I consider 12 points to be a difference that is worthy of explanation. (p. 24)

On fluctuations within the Verbal and Performance Scales:

> I believe the 5% level of significance is quite adequate for investigating the WISC-R profile. . . . Furthermore, I would encourage examiners to use a constant difference of ± 3 points from the child's Verbal or Performance mean scaled score to determine the significance of the deviation of *any* subtest. (p. 54)

1990 Revision of the Second Rule:[b]

> The values of approximately ± 3 do not take into account the errors that occur when multiple comparisons are made at once. When the Bonferroni corrections are made, the ± 3 rule no longer holds for the WISC-R (it does, however, hold for the WAIS-R). For the WISC-R, the best rule of thumb is ± 3 for all six Verbal subtests and Block Design; and ± 4 for the remaining Performance subtests. (Personal communication, March 21, 1990)

---

[a]From *Intelligent Testing with the WISC-R* by A. S. Kaufman, 1979. New York: Wiley. Copyright 1979 by John Wiley and Sons. Reprinted by permission.
[b]A. S. Kaufman, personal communication, March 21, 1990.

rules yield slightly different results than cumbersome formulas. In Jason's case, that slight difference crosses the boundary of significance; and, the practitioner's figuring shows statistical significance, but the more complex calculation does not. Jason's Coding score is 3 points below his Performance average, significantly low by the practitioners' rules; but the difference needed for a 5% level of significance by more precise means is 3.2 (Kaufman, 1979, p. 55)!

Those who are more accustomed to working with probabilities than most practitioners might say that the difference between 3 points and

3.2 points is a difference in degree (and a slight degree, at that), not in kind; if 3.2 points is significant at the 5% level, then 3 points is significant at only a slightly less acceptable level, say around 6%.

The practitioner need not feel outclassed. Working rules are essential practitioner equipment. No one should fret over 0.2 of a scaled score point. Slight inaccuracies are more than compensated for by having the test interpreted by someone who majored in child psychology instead of statistics.

Example 1-4 shows the Level 2 interpretation of Jason's examination. In Example 1-4, conclusions are drawn from the statistical significance of the differences among scores in Jason's test profile. Differences are interpreted according to both the subtest equivalencies seen in Level 1 and empirical research about test factors and score patterns in various populations.

The significantly low Coding score (W denotes "weak") prompts a list of possible reasons, but no commitment on the best choice. Although hedging is at times unavoidable, consultees look to the examiner for definitive answers to their questions.

The report concludes that the test results would explain difficulties in writing and spelling. Jason is also underachieving in reading, but the report does not discuss whether a broader reason might affect all three. Table 3 compares characteristics of Level 1 and Level 2.

There is an important part missing from this picture. What part is missing?

Jason is missing from the picture. Even his description is taken from a checklist of a handful of standard categories and not integrated into a unified picture. There are categories and factors, possibilities and probabilities, but Jason is nowhere to be seen.

Table 3
Comparison of Level 1 and Level 2

Level 1	Level 2
Concrete	Mechanical
Does not draw conclusions	Draws conclusions from scores alone
Test-centered	Population-centered
Descriptive	Prescriptive
Enumerative	Statistical
Laundry List	Cookbook

Example 1-4

Name: Jason
Age: 10-8

Test Results:

Wechsler Intelligence Scale for Children — Revised

Verbal Tests		Performance Tests	
Information	10	Picture Completion	12
Similarities	8	Picture Arrangement	11
Arithmetic	9	Block Design	11
Vocabulary	9	Object Assembly	13
Comprehension	10	Coding	8 W
(Digit Span)	(7)		

Verbal Scale IQ	95	Performance Scale IQ	106
	Full Scale IQ	100	

Discussion:

Jason was clean and neatly dressed. He was attentive and cooperative. He related appropriately to the examiner and appeared to try his best on all assigned tasks. The results of this examination are considered valid.

The difference between Jason's Verbal Scale IQ and Performance Scale IQ does not reach the level of statistical significance.

Subtest clusters do not show any factor indicating deficiencies.

None of the verbal subtests differs significantly from the mean of the verbal subtests.

The Coding subtest is significantly lower than the mean of the performance subtests. There are a number of possible weaknesses associated with a low Coding score. These include deficiency in visual-motor coordination; low visual-motor speed; deficiency in pencil skills, which often shows in difficulties in handwriting and written expression; low visual short-term memory, which may show in difficulty copying from the blackboard and learning spelling words; difficulty attending and concentrating; and low motivation on rote-learning and clerical tasks.

Although the Coding score, with its possible implications for the learning tasks listed above, is consistent with some learning problems, the profile as a whole is not strongly indicative of learning disabilities.

Example 1-5

Jason, 10-8

WISC-R Test Results:

Verbal Tests		Performance Tests	
Information	10	Picture Completion	12
Similarities	8	Picture Arrangement	11
Arithmetic	9	Block Design	11
Vocabulary	9	Object Assembly	13
Comprehension	10	Coding	8 W
(Digit Span)	(7)		

Verbal Scale IQ	95	Performance Scale IQ	106
	Full Scale IQ	100	

Discussion of WISC-R:

Jason is at least 5 feet tall, mature, well-oriented, realistic, . . .

. . . and attentive. He dislikes needing special services, and felt negative about being tested, but nevertheless cooperated thoroughly. He is extremely competitive and self-motivated on tasks he can succeed on.

LEVEL 3.
THE INDIVIDUALIZED LEVEL: JASON REVEALED

The individualized level of interpretation puts Jason back in the picture with specific details and events that characterize him and no one else.

← Instead of launching immediately into an interpretation of these scores, as in Levels 1 and 2, Level 3 suspends judgment until the behavioral data are considered.

← The first sentence has the customary introductory thumbnail description. At first it might seem to be more for the benefit of the examiner and administrators, as the parents and teachers already know how he looks and acts. But besides tying the report to a real person, physical descriptions have implications for conclusions and recommendations. Jason's height, for example, suggests that he is already in pre-adolescence, and special services ought to consider his needs for autonomy and preserving appearances.

← The attention and motivation mentioned have some bearing on the test validity. It is not necessary to mention validity specifically if it is obvious from the context. In this case, validity resurfaces later when background material is introduced and findings summarized.

The attention and motivation also speak for Jason's character. He comes through the layers of semi-technical language as an admirable person, irrespective of age.

Physical appearance, attention, and general motivation flesh out the picture, but these alone do not lead to individualized diagnostic conclusions because they do not bear directly on school learning, except to suggest that he is better motivated on some tasks than others, and the tasks that motivate him are not specified.

Example 1-5 *(continued)*

Although the only significantly weak WISC-R subtest score is Coding, Jason's behavior showed many learning discrepancies.

He is an excellent listener when the stimulus is clear-cut, but has difficulty understanding complex language. He remembers many facts that are meaningfully embedded for him, but has difficulty remembering arbitrary or meaningless facts (states, numbers). He has excellent practical understanding but has difficulty expressing himself in language on the level of his understanding.

His holistic (global) performance on hand-eye tasks is consistent with being left-handed with a hooked pencil-hold. Lack of analysis and attention to detail is partly his style, and partly the result of over-confidence in his considerable holistic abilities.

Example 1-5 *(continued)*

Jason's many learning disabilities, most of which do not show up in the test profile, and the quality of some of his responses, suggest that he is brighter than his present IQ scores show.

The drop in scores since his last test often accompanies a learning disability, as the test content becomes increasingly school-influenced with age.

← The lead-in prepares the test-wise reader for information that suggests conclusions different from Levels 1 and 2.

← Strengths get as much mention as weaknesses. Small characteristics are mentioned if judged relevant.

The description of Jason's learning characteristics is outlined but not documented.

A qualified professional is not required to explain the rationale for every diagnostic conclusion in writing. This report reflects the reality rather than the ideal report. The women's movement has called attention to women's feelings of inadequacy in comparison to an unrealistic ideal, but despair over this kind of disparity plagues every group, including practitioners. The long, elegant reports in textbooks are a good teaching device but are hardly practical for examiners with busy schedules. Questions can be answered in person at the evaluation meeting from notes and protocols. The data and reasoning behind this description of Jason's learning characteristics appear in full as an example of the reasoning process in Chapter 4, pp. 109-129. Political implications of requiring complete documentation are discussed in Chapter 6, p. 182.

← The description of Jason's learning characteristics leads to a re-evaluation of the validity of the test scores. This is *internal* evidence instead of the external factors of attention, cooperation, and motivation.

← The explanation of the difference between past and present test scores is the exception rather than the custom among test reports, most of which consider only the present test. The examiner's task is to explain the whole picture, and the previous examiner is probably no less competent than the present one. There is a tendency for test scores of children with learning problems to drop over time, and IQ-conscious parents need some explanation.

The proof of the pudding is in the eating, and the proof of a learning disability is in the academic achievements.

Example 1-5 *(continued)*

Jason, 10-8, Grade 4

Achievements:

Reading:	Grade Equivalent	Percentile Rank	Standard Score
Decoding: WRAT-R, Level 1	2 Mid.	1	65

Comprehension: New Sucher-Allred Reading Placement Inventory
  Instructional Level: Grade 1
  Frustration Level: Grade 2
  See comments under Discussion below

Written Expression:

Spelling: WRAT-R, Level 1	2 Beg.	2	69

Writing sample, criterion-referenced, using standards from the local curriculum
  Capitalization: Inconsistent mastery of first word (grade 1)
  Expression: Beginning grade 3
    Writes and recognizes complete sentence (grade 2+)
    Writes short story in proper sequence (grade 2+)
  Language: Below thought level shown elsewhere (grade 2 to 3)
  Handwriting: Uses cursive script (grade 4)

Math: Criterion-referenced, using examples from the Brigance Inventory of Basic Skills, and standards from local curriculum: Grade 4, gap at grade 3
  Multidigit subtraction with borrowing (grade 3+)
  Multiplication facts need refreshing (grade 3)
  Multiplies 3 digits × 1 digit with carrying (grade 4)

Discussion of Achievements:

Decoding is a serious problem for Jason. He missequences sounds on some one-syllable words (*felt*), and has difficulty with two-syllable words. He says he has enjoyed reading sports books. Reading comprehension is severely limited by decoding. He shows excellent comprehension, and high goals in making up titles that summarize the story, on a grade 3 reading level; but inability to decode key words caused him to fail to answer a passing number of comprehension questions above the grade-1 level.

Written expression is affected by oral language expression difficulties. His holistic style is not compatible with being a good speller.

The Level 2 report, Example 1-4, offered one hypothesis, based on the low Coding score, of a pencil deficiency that might produce difficulties in handwriting and written expression. To test that hypothesis, Figure 2 shows Jason's writing sample from the evaluation of his written expression. Although the lines slant downward, for Jason to write in cursive script this neatly and fluidly, on unlined paper, shortly after the introduction of cursive, suggests that at present pencil skills are not a major concern.

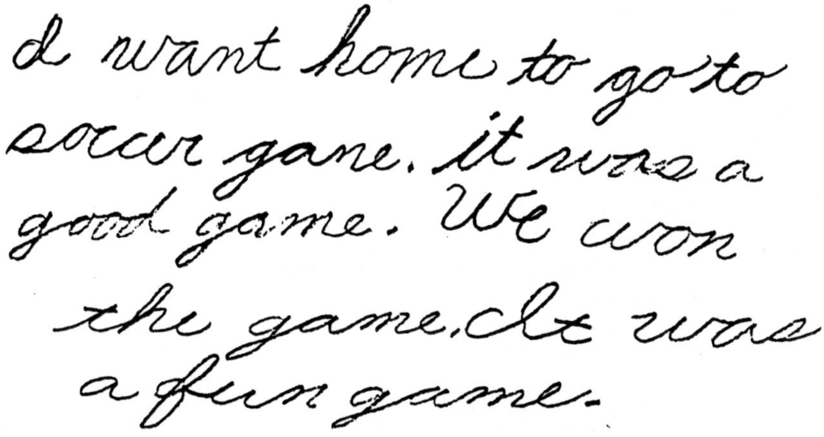

Figure 2. Jason's writing sample.

Tests are not given in a vacuum. There must be a reason for referral, and background information is often relevant. This reason for referral changes the picture from the start, because it tells that Jason has been identified as a problem learner for several years, and we do not begin with a blank slate.

Example 1-5 *(continued)*

Reason for Referral: Re-evaluation every 3 years to determine continued eligibility for special services.

Background Information:

Early Development and Medical: Jason's mother was prescribed medication for difficulties during pregnancy. Jason was born in the posterior presentation. At 2 years, a fall caused a cut on the forehead,

(continued)

Example 1-5 *(continued)*

but he did not lose consciousness. At 2½ he had a high fever without convulsions. Developmental milestones were normal.

When Jason was 7-5, an optometrist found normal eyesight, but "multisensory difficulties that made school difficult."

When he was 8-1, a pediatric neurologist diagnosed developmental dyslexia.

Family: Jason and his sister, 12, live with their parents, who are both employed.

Activities, Interests: Jason enjoys playing basketball, baseball, and soccer. He likes to build things with batteries that make light bulbs light.

School History:

In kindergarten, he "needed to work on motor skills." [This usually refers to crayons, pencil, and scissors.] He was coded learning disabled at the end of grade 1, and has remained so ever since. Services have included speech/language. In grade 2, his language-related tool skills were moved to the resource room. He now spends 7.5 hours a week there.

He does especially well on science projects, and just earned an A on one.

Previous Tests:

Age 6-2, at his preschool screening, Jason failed the Preschool Speech and Language Test. The Gesell School Readiness Test found immature fine motor skills.

Age 7-7, on a WISC-R, Jason scored VSIQ 113, PSIQ 123, and FSIQ 120; with significant strengths in Vocabulary and Mazes, and significant weaknesses in Digit Span and Picture Completion. A speech and language examination at that time showed age-appropriate vocabulary and concepts, but a 1-year lag in language processing and expressive language.

Summary: Jason is a bright boy who is a successful math and science student, a strong thinker, self-motivated where he can succeed, and may be creative; but he has a language-based learning disability, with difficulties in comprehension of complex language and in oral expression on his thought level. In addition, his holistic learning style, which is an asset in mechanics and science, causes difficulty in sequential processes in reading and spelling. His strengths have obscured his learning disabilities in the present WISC-R profile. He is underachieving 3 years in language-related tool skills.

Despite the uninteresting WISC-R profile — the lack of those vaunted "peaks and valleys" — Jason is a student who would be identified as learning disabled even in the most economy-minded and least service-oriented district.

The reason for the difference between the conclusions of Level 2 and Level 3 is that tests are samples of behavior, chosen to represent certain content. In some cases, the sampling process misses its target, but the targeted content is expressed in other behaviors that are not scored. This situation may be more common in the referred population, which might be expected to respond to school-related tasks in nonconforming ways.

Figure 3. "Oh well, another day's digging shot to hell." Reprinted Courtesy OMNI Magazine © 1990.

This story has two morals. The first is, in order to find something, it is necessary to look in the right place. Figure 3 illustrates this point. The second is, it is necessary to look at the scores through the child rather than at the child through the scores. The *part* of the child to look at the scores through is the child's *learning-related test behavior*.

Table 4 compares the three levels of interpretation discussed in this chapter.

Table 4
Comparison of Level 1, Level 2, and Level 3

	Level 1	Level 2	Level 3
	Concrete	Mechanical	Individualized
Inferential scope	Does not draw conclusions	Draws conclusions from scores alone	Draws conclusions from scores, behavior, and background
Content	Test-centered	Population-centered	Subject-centered
Activity	Descriptive	Prescriptive	Explanatory
Numerical approach	Enumerative	Statistical	Qualitative
Metaphor	Laundry list	Cookbook	Handbook

2 THE DESCRIPTION OF TEST BEHAVIOR

Description of test behavior is a necessary step in drawing conclusions from tests. *Description* is separate from *observation*. Observation is a solitary act of perception, whereas description is putting that perception into a shared language, however spontaneously worded or illegibly scrawled.

There are three topics that will *not* be discussed at length: writing reports, objective reporting of behavior, and how not to give offense.

1. *Writing reports.* This book is about reasoning, not writing. Examples are taken from reports because reports are the means of communication about clinical reasoning.

Thinking is a necessary part of writing, and clarifying one's thinking will make writing clearer, as well. But the relationship is two-sided. Thoughts are so fluid that writing them down is often the easiest way to begin clarifying them.

Clarification of thinking is not a purely solitary activity. It implies that an audience will eventually be out there. The characteristics of the intended audience shape the spinning-out of the thinking process. Practitioners learn by experience the kinds of reasons their colleagues accept, the kinds they applaud.

Writing carries much additional baggage, from struggles to control a pencil at age 5 or 6, through judgments of second-grade teachers about handwriting and fifth-grade teachers about usage, to problems with thesis advisors and the recipients of love letters. Therefore writing is a separate skill, best improved through individual feedback. Examiners who are not much interested in writing can take comfort in Gerald Caplan's (1970, p. 260) comment that a psychological report is a business document, not a literary one.

2. *Objective reporting of behavior.* Description of behavior inevitably raises that old bugbear, *Psych* or *Child Dev 101,* the course that taught Observation of Behavior. Its purpose was to teach beginning students both to observe behavior and to distinguish between their observations and their naive interpretations. It is assumed here that before students approach testing, they have already learned how to observe behavior, and that subsequent courses and experience replace naive interpretations with professional ones. Therefore, practitioners need not maintain the distinction between observation and interpretation in their daily work. There is a great deal to do in giving a test, and it is more efficient to jot down whatever comes to mind, often an interpretation. A practitioner's behavioral notes are broken into observation and interpretation in Chapter 4.

The enduring lesson of *101* is that a distinction between observation and interpretation remains, and at some time it may be necessary to replace one interpretation with another as individual or scientific horizons expand to include new knowledge. It is ideal, though not always possible, to keep somewhere a memory trace of the original behavior for such occasions.

The examples of description of test behavior in this chapter are a mix of observations, interpretations, and more general conclusions, whichever one seemed the most expedient way to record them at the time.

3. *How not to give offense.* This is part of consultation and writing, not thinking. It is intended to be demonstrated but not discussed. One gradually absorbs layers of euphemisms as last year's scientific terminology biodegrades into this year's slurs ("moron," "retarded," "developmentally disabled"). This writer learned the skill working in the Chicago Public Schools. In those days, all the school psychologists who were in the office on the same day sat around one big table writing reports. Occasionally someone would say, "How do you say . . . ?" and someone would answer.[1] But there is a price for learning to blunt the truth. School psychologists hardly ever write really good novels.[2]

The descriptions of test behavior in this chapter are taken from my reports over a 6-year period, with the addition of three particularly memorable previous incidents. The total number of reports sampled was approximately 320 learning evaluations, some of which also included personality assessments, and about 48 achievement evaluations. Most were done in public schools, a few in private schools, and 30 achievement evaluations were done in the adolescent department of a psychiatric hospital.

On ready-made categories.   The examples in this chapter are all taken from narrative records, not from observation techniques that use ready-made categories. The ability to use the free-style narrative technique requires the observer to have already mastered a number of relevant sets of categories.

Although the remarks below were made in response to ready-made *behavioral* categories, they apply equally well to any set of ready-made categories, whether of behavior, interpretation, or solutions.

Categories are a necessity in thinking. The examiner's education and experience should have provided these. A major plank in the viewpoint expressed in this book is that examiners should be free to use those categories they find most useful. Sets of ready-made categories are helpful to students learning the choices available, and in behavior modification, research data gathering, and statistical reportage, but they are not suitable to impose on independent practitioners for evaluations. Ready-made, supposedly complete sets of categories limit examiners' ability to use their skills and knowledge to the fullest and stunt their capacity for further professional growth. No set of categories can provide for all occasions until knowledge is complete and final, and everything there is to know is already known. That would mean a complete, perfect model of human learning. It is a basic tenet of modern science that knowledge is never finished or perfect, and there are always new discoveries to be made. A more subtle and condescending assumption of closed sets of categories is that practitioners are not worthy to provide new insights or make contributions to science. (The importance of freedom to choose one's own categories is also discussed in Chapter 6, pp. 174, 182).

AREAS OF TEST BEHAVIOR

The examples in this chapter are grouped into such areas as *appearance, situation, relationship with the examiner,* and so on. Many of these areas are also subdivided into smaller areas or facets that may hold diagnostic information. Appearance includes *general description, defining details, expression, clothing, developmental stage,* and more.

These areas and facets are not intended to burden examiners with a list of items that must be noted, but to point out the many possible sources of information about how the person functions in a learning situation.

The areas are presented in the traditional test-report order, beginning with the physical description, which is discovered first, and moving toward the learning behavior being tested, which is usually discovered last. Language behavior occurs throughout the testing session. It is observed second only to appearance, but the full implications of its relationship to learning often do not appear until the actual test responses. Although behavior observed later in the session is usually more intrinsically related to learning, all facets of behavior, and even appearance, sometimes have implications for learning.

Appearance

Physical descriptions serve at least five purposes:

1. They begin by recognizing the most apparent and familiar aspect of the child's individuality. This purpose is well-captured by Linda Walbridge's[3] (personal communication, June, 1976) direction to her department members that a description should tell how that person looks different from other people.

2. They help the examiner remember the child apart from other children tested. One psychiatrist[4] took Polaroid pictures of all his patients, in both mental health center and private practice, for nearly two decades. The patients showed permission by signing the pictures. These complemented his notes to help him recapture the whole person.

3. Physical characteristics can be considered a part of behavior to the extent that the form of anything is the result of some past motion or force (Thompson, 1917/1961). Appearance sometimes holds a clue to differences in development or behavior that bear on the question at hand.

4. Appearance plays a large part in determining how a person will be treated by others and therefore provides information about social assets and liabilities.

5. Physical characteristics are the view of the child the examiner most certainly shares with those who come from a different perspective — teachers and parents; and this shared perception provides a bond between them. The goal of an examination is a new perception of puzzling or troubling behaviors;[5] but, such change can be threatening. The more agreement at the beginning of the chain of reasoning, the greater likelihood of acceptance of the differing perception in conclusion.

General Descriptions and Distinctive Details

Descriptions can sum up the general look, or present details that define or set apart.

[Age 5-10] He is an adorable, cherubic-looking small boy with immature pronunciation.

[4-8] She is a solid little girl wearing a patch on her right eye. She is the larger and more assertive of the twins.

[6-3] He had unevenly cut hair and a rough-and-ready look.

[6-8] She had the sweetly bossy manner of many little girls who have younger brothers.

[9-7] He looks overwhelmed by large glasses he seems to balance carefully.

[16-6] He differs from many persons with Down's Syndrome by his long head, red hair, and tuft of chin-whiskers.

Expression

Sometimes the person's facial expression stands out as distinctive.

[11-7] He is a small, preadolescent boy whose eyes gleam with friendliness and enthusiasm.

[9-4] He is a chunky, small boy with an infectious smile and warmth following his initial prolonged look of puzzlement.

[9-8] She has a humorously expressive face and, even when dressed-up, has a wholesome, unselfconscious, outdoor quality.

[14-0] His expression in repose is a frown.

[10-2] Her "poker" expression becomes smiling and responsive when she discusses personal concerns.

Clothing

Clothing can be memorable as well as characteristic.

[8-1] He was clean and neatly dressed in country clothing.

[11-3] She wore a jaunty sweatsuit on an October day that had turned unseasonably warm.

[9-11] She is a pleasant-looking, slender, preadolescent girl who is very clean and has the hastily assembled look typical of her age.

[13-9] His appearance combines efforts at swashbuckle (styled hair, single earring, braided wrist-cords) with lack of grooming (needed haircut and general improvement).

[17-10] He is a personable young man with a flair for casual style.

Developmental Stage

The developmental stage can be an especially important element during periods of rapid change — the early years of school, and the course of adolescence.

[6-9] Her size is appropriate for her age, but her features are those of a kindergartner.

[6-8] Her well-defined features and self-possessed mien make her seem mature.

[8-7] She is a tall girl in whom the unselfconsciousness and flyaway grooming of the young child contrast sharply with her beauty and preadolescent developmental maturity.

[9-10] He is a tall, well-proportioned boy who looks 2 years older than his age.

[11-6] He is small for his age, but there is maturity in his intense facial expression.

[14-5] She is a physically mature girl who could be taken for an adult, but her dress and manner are appropriate for early teen-age.

Signs of a Way of Life

Appearance can suggest a way of life.

[8-6] His appearance has traces of an active outdoor life.

[15-1] This pretty girl with streaked ringlets looks like the social butterfly that everyone, including herself, says she is.

[9-0] This well-grown girl was trying to look grown-up that day and had adopted one item rather than attending to general grooming. The item was mother's boots, and they hurt.

[10-10] He is a large, pleasant, smiling boy reminiscent of the children one used to meet in isolated rural schools. He had started the day clean and neat. In the morning session his hands had gotten dirty since he left home, and by the afternoon session, his face too.

[17-1] He is an attractive, somber, intense, masculine person who immediately comes across as not comfortable in harness, and in need of space.

Signs of Problems

Appearance can provide the first clue to problems.

[3-1] She is a diminutive, attractive child about the size of a 1-year old.

[10-9] The lower part of his face is asymmetrical, and when he talks all his features grimace, as though he cannot execute finely differentiated facial movements.

[7-5] He is a small, bright-eyed boy with irregularly shaped ears, and facial scars.

[15-5] He is a small, quiet boy, lacking the spontaneity and expression of aggression we usually see in boys this age.

[13-4] His hands are large, and the side of his dominant left hand was covered with graphite from rubbing over his own pencil writing. We had to start by washing his hands to protect the test materials.

[17-3] A large crystal pendant on a thong around his neck was called inappropriate by his teacher, especially when she recalled that he had worn it with his ROTC uniform.

The above snippets raise questions, respectively, about developmental delay, neurological soundness, birth injury and family abuse, emotional adjustment, mastery of primary grade basic skills, and capacity for the most rudimentary conformity to even voluntary organizations.

The Appearance of Handicaps

The obviousness of physical and mental handicaps affects the degree to which they are also social handicaps.

[9-7] She is a pleasant-looking, ladylike girl in latency. Her mobility handicap causes her to walk a bit more slowly than the average child and might be a social handicap with peers until a relationship is formed.

[6-7] He is tall for his age, and has regular features and an appropriate social smile. Sometimes he walks with normal gait, but at other times with exaggerated, less-controlled motion. The difference in his appearance consists of behavior. He shows effort in attending by grimacing, cocking his head, and off-center body posture.

[14-1] This large, obese boy with a habitual grin always wears a stocking cap pulled halfway down over his forehead indoors. His appearance calls attention to him as different.

[19-11] He has craggy but regular features and was a bit rumpled, but generally appropriate in appearance.

[17-1] She is a tall, slender girl of appropriate physical development and grooming, who moves gracefully and does not have any marks of retardation.

These appearances can suggest activities and goals. The students might benefit, respectively, from a social group activity, gross motor training, basic hygiene and social skills, survival housekeeping skills, and supervision of the social activities of a young woman whose appearance gives no warning of her moderate retardation.

Situation

Once in a while, before the student even makes an appearance, events have set the stage. This pretest behavior is a pertinent sample of the student's life in conjunction with testing.

[17-1] He was relieved to be rescued from the tedium of in-school suspension by being tested. The suspension was not an isolated occurrence.

[8-2] He was tested on three different days. On the third, his parents said he refused to come to school. The police brought him in not long before the session.

[12-10] Earlier in the year I was asked to test this boy's older brother to relieve the heavy workload of Mr. Currier, who is both boys' counselor and favorite school person. The older brother refused to see me, and Mr. Currier administered his test. Now I was asked to test the younger brother, who also refused. It was suggested to him that the natural consequence of not taking a 3-year update examination is to be thrown back into the mainstream. Faced with this possibility, he agreed to take the test from me.

[15-7] When I asked for him in the office, he was on out-of-school suspension for punching another student in class, between the bell and the teacher's arrival.

Relationship with the Examiner

A Sample Relationship

The relationship the subject sets up with the examiner encapsulates the way the subject meets the world.

[5-7] She is secure and comfortable with people.

[9-1] She hung back a bit about coming with me.

[14-6] He is placid and unaffectedly polite, appropriate in relating to authority, frank about his feelings and able to joke about his failings, and altogether a delightful person.

[19-11] He became inappropriately personal, touching this older examiner and asking if she were married, in a needy rather than aggressive way.

[17-5] He ended the session by complimenting the examiner for establishing rapport with him — a system-wise subject.

These samples show, respectively, a child with good interpersonal skills; a shy or reluctant one; a positive and well-adjusted teen-ager; a young man whose lack of emotional outlets leads to behavior that might get him into social difficulties; and one who tries to manipulate and change places with authority. The latter had had some difficulties with the law and some success in rehabilitation, and had not yet decided which side he was on.

Signs of Problems

The relationship with the examiner sometimes immediately signals difficulties.

[5-4] She did not look directly at me for 15 minutes, giving a trance-like impression. It was difficult for her to walk with me in the hall without wandering off. Despite these hitches, she was an agreeable, cooperative child.

This child's interpersonal behavior was sometimes unusual and anxiety provoking. A personality evaluation supported the *agreeable, cooperative* side in finding that her problems were not primarily emotional, but might lie in constitutional factors.

[7-5] He sets up a relationship with authority in which he tries to communicate his feelings and needs by indirect means, apparently to avoid causing anger. The result is so irritating that he provokes the very anger he seeks to avoid. He asks permission when it is not necessary. He expresses annoyance with himself first, to keep the other person from doing so. He presents himself as a victim. He answers questions so backhandedly that it is hard to understand his meaning.

[7-6] Her behavior has a babyish quality. She whined to stop working. She can get into a subtle, dependent tug-of-war with an adult.

These children's behavior reflected their response to adult authority in troubled homes. The first was caught between abusive male and victimized female family members, the second in a custody battle between parents with handicaps of their own.

[13-10] He immediately set up a negative relationship. He was not in the room he was scheduled for and did not come to my office as his teacher directed. He used his legitimate auditory problems to avoid and antagonize, by constantly saying, "Huh?" When I asked why he had moved to our town, he answered, "None o' ya business."

[17-2] He expressed initial unwillingness to take part in the examination, but did come with me. However, he expressed increasing discomfort and suspiciousness about the situation, and finally walked out.

The last two had long been identified as having serious emotional and behavioral problems. The last, in addition, was having an immediate mental health crisis.

The Examiner's Response

To every action there is an equal and opposite reaction. Sometimes the examiner's participation is an intrinsic part of the subject's test behavior.

> [14-11, referred for school phobia] He was cooperative and worked well, but asked early to go to lunch. I kept his jacket.

> [5-1, referred the first week of kindergarten] I had a hard time getting compliance. He began crying after we exchanged a few sentences. At his teacher's insistence, he completed the test with me in a corner of the kindergarten, but after 15 minutes he became negative, cried, "My mommy," lay on the floor, and kicked a flannel board over so that it fell on top of both of us.

> [6-3] She had been seeing the school counselor for individual attention and did not want to leave him to come with me. He stayed with us during the session. She sat on his lap, and when he left for an instant, she wailed after him, calling him by the wrong name, the principal's name. She kept backing her chair away from the test materials. On a trip to the lavatory, she locked herself into a toilet stall. I had to pull her out by the legs from below the stall door, and carry her wriggling back to her classroom.

It would be difficult to give the flavor of these three students' behavior without mentioning the examiner's involvement.

The Examiner's Intervention

The examiner's intervention or restructuring of the test situation can show what is needed to get the child to perform and may serve as a springboard for programming.

> [3-2] He constantly explored the attractive school toys and asserted his autonomy. By following him around the floor, pleasantly demanding his attention, and feeding him rice cereal, I was able to complete the Stanford-Binet.

This child, a home behavior problem, was referred by his physician. He was placed in a preschool program with the same combination of nurturant acceptance and insistent structure shown in the examiner's intervention.

[6-9, referred for elective mutism] His teacher suggested we work in a corner of her classroom behind a screen, and had prepared him and explained that he wouldn't have to talk to me. He still refused to come. She told him he could not join the group until he did, leaving him alone a few yards from my desk. I called out, offering him a raisin to come and sit with me. He crawled under the nearest desk.

I sat on the floor near him, with the Wechsler Object Assembly sample puzzle arranged on my clipboard, and told him I would show him how to do the puzzle; and if he did it after me, I would give him a raisin. He appeared more interested in the puzzle than the raisin, and did one and accepted the other. In the same vein, he came and sat at the table, and we completed all the nonverbal tests available. After 20 minutes, during which it was made clear he did not have to talk, he began to talk to me.

After several years of encouragement, language therapy, and tutoring, this boy is far more responsive. His learning problem has turned out to be far more serious than was recognized at the time. His expectancy then for beginning level work did not provide much opportunity for a discrepancy, and he refused to cooperate in his weak area, expression.

Attention

Qualities of Attention

The qualities of subjects' attention have great educational relevance: whether they focus, maintain attention, attend better to some kinds of things than others, and are distracted by external or internal stimuli.

[5-4] She worked well for two 1-hour sessions.

[7-5] She is able to focus her attention, but does not sustain it for more than a second.

[6-7] Differential success among kinds of tasks appears to be due more to attentional variation than to intrinsic differences among abilities. Colorful materials hold his attention better than black-and-white.

[5-11] He was distracted by the visual qualities of the materials, and did what they suggested instead of what I told him to do. Told to draw a line like mine, he drew one that crossed mine instead.

[8-7] She is distracted by her own associations to questions asked.

[16-5] She has difficulty shutting her feelings and personal life out of her mind at school time.

Attention Deficit

The other side of attention is attention deficit. Attention deficit can be educationally devastating. Norman Garmezy said, "Attentional dysfunction is the substrate out of which incompetence arises" (Pines, 1975). Test behavior provides clues to attention deficit and can be highly indicative; but conclusive diagnosis requires specialized techniques beyond observation in this one situation.

[12-7] He showed a high degree of distractibility and impulsiveness.

[8-0] He notices tiny, far-off, irrelevant details more than material presented to him.

[6-8] Most observations about his test behavior concern attentional deficit, hyperactivity, impulsivity, and lack of focus, which greatly affected test results. He immediately began exploring the testing room, noticed things outside the window, brought a small object out of his pocket to play with, and kept bringing up other things he wanted to do besides what we were doing. He could be controlled by the relationship between us.

[13-7] He showed excellent attention, with residual traces of his earlier behavior in very rapid thinking, answering right away or not at all, getting up in his seat, and playing with the stapler. None of this interfered with his application.

The first two selections provide clues consistent with attentional deficit. The third is highly indicative. The fourth describes a recovering or rehabilitated sufferer who still displays mild physical accompaniments, but his attention—in this one-to-one situation—is excellent.

Two cases of attention deficit appear in Chapter 5, pp. 154-161.

Motivation

Amount of Motivation

Test subjects differ in degree of motivation. Here are two well-motivated, one overly motivated, and two negatively motivated subjects.

[10-5] He was extra conscientious and plugged away valiantly at tasks that were the most difficult for him.

[8-5] Self-motivation and persistence were above average.

[8-5] He is a highly motivated, competitive child, who tends to jump the gun and take shortcuts; the intensity of his efforts is sometimes counterproductive.

[11-8] His attitude was passive endurance rather than active participation.

[11-11] When asked to do math, she cried.

Source of Motivation

Some students work to please others, whereas others are "in business for themselves." Some are motivated by success, and others by intrinsic interest in learning.

[13-10] He was motivated, but clearly working only for external authorities.

[17-11] He was motivated for his own sake rather than mine.

[12-11] She has internal standards for effort and application.

[14-3] His best quality is his achievement motivation, perhaps not in the sense of interest, but wanting to compete and succeed.

[7-1] Her motivation and enthusiasm for learning are a great asset. She was delighted to read the abbreviation of *oz.* on her juice carton, "Oz" [as in *The Wizard of Oz*], and volunteered to write a long list of family given names she had just learned.

Differential Motivation

Motivation can be different for different tasks. Here are some students with differential motivation for understanding, problem solving, game-like tasks, creativity, a hand–eye task, and expression of emotions.

[16-4] He has a strong need for closure and understanding of material presented to him.

[11-3] She enjoys a thinking-cap challenge.

[14-5] He enjoyed the competitive challenge of the Binet [4th ed.] puzzle format.

[7-2] She loves to read, enjoyed writing a story and in general creating things.

[10-4] She does not put forth much effort on verbal and academic tasks, but was quite motivated on Kaufman's Triangles [hand–eye subtest of the K-ABC].

[14-5] She had low motivation on the IQ and achievement tests, but responded very fully to projective techniques.

The Examiner as Motivator

When motivation is negative, the examiner can sometimes provide the external motivation needed for a valid examination. Direct insistence worked with the first youngster below, but the second required a more elaborate structure, which might later serve as a model for his program.

[11-10] He has his own achievement goals, which do not include the ones we set for him. In fact, he expends a great deal of energy on diversion tactics to prevent school adults from presenting him with work, and can be remarkably dominant and persuasive about it. When forced to work, he has a lively, questioning mind, and readily projects himself into the material.

[8-0] During the first session, he put forth minimal effort, and expressed great impatience with the proceedings. "How long do I have to stay? How many things do I have to do? Do I have to do both sides [of the page]?" He acted impulsive and touched things.

In the middle of a lackluster effort, I said in desperation, "Do it like you're doing it for yourself instead of for me." His eyes grew bright. He said, "O-o-oh! Doing it for *myself*!" He redoubled his efforts and achieved greater success.

The second session I offered a small reward (he chose pennies over raisins) for each time he "really tried," regardless of correctness. He did not understand that the reward was for application, not success, but his attention improved greatly.

Language

Language behavior unfolds throughout the examination, from the initial social conversation to the more school-like uses of language. In younger children, language is closely tied in with global development. Young children usually produce their best language early in the session in response to homey, familiar, rapport-building topics like their family and pets. Older children often reveal more about their language in the stress of the actual test.

In view of the pervasiveness of language deficits among delayed readers (see Stanovich, 1986), language behavior is a highly important category of test behavior intrinsically related to learning. Although language is the province of its own specialists, other examiners can describe language in a nontechnical way that both helps language specialists judge the need for their own further involvement and contributes to the identification of language learning disabilities.

Language has many aspects that might strike a language nonspecialist as relevant to the purposes of the examination:

Diction

Pronunciation can be one clue to developmental level in beginning schoolchildren, as in the first illustration under *General Description*, p. 25. Like *Appearance* (p. 27), it can be a factor in the obviousness of handicaps:

> [14-6] He has good diction, and despite a low Verbal IQ, carries on conversation well and had a fund of information about his family.

> [19-11] He expresses himself readily, but his speech, which has sound substitutions that give a "thick" effect, immediately stigmatizes him.

Expression in General Conversation

Some students show their language characteristics most clearly when they choose their own topic.

> [7-10] Language and cognition are mature. He used such terms as "ammunition" and "Terrible Twos," made logical distinctions, and described complex family relationships not usually understood by little boys.

> [9-8] He likes to talk, but his speech is rambling and infantile. ("He fell down. Poor Johny-John. Tsk-tsk-tsk.") Content was sometimes inappropriate (said he couldn't wait till he was 18 to pick on kids, hide in the bushes and scare them).

> [10-9] He is a direct, realistic informant, and what his language lacks in elegance, it makes up in informational content.

> [15-3] He differs from many high school students coded learning disabled in having good speech and being spontaneously verbally and emotionally expressive. He offers information such as details of his early school history and explanations of life in general.

Expression in Test Responses

Some students reveal most about their language abilities when they answer test questions.

> [7-11] His language is vague, and he has difficulty with definitions and explanations. His solution is to give lengthy responses that do not squarely answer the question.

> [13-5] Her intellectual development can be seen from her spontaneous multiple responses on verbal subtests and her ability to define words in parallel grammatic form.

[13-8] There is sometimes an uneven quality to his expression, both oral and written, which is the result of his effort to achieve the truest meaning through alternative explanations and high levels of abstraction, rather than being glib and simplistic.

[17-10] His nonverbal communication is so good as to obscure his language deficiency. One has to write down his answers to see how vague, impoverished, and concrete they are, because he makes them sound adequate.

Receptive Language

Sometimes receptive language comes to the fore.

[6-8] He is an excellent listener.

[6-11] She has excellent language expression, including vocabulary, but she had some difficulty understanding my conversation and directions. As our mode became more auditory, she became slightly restless and inattentive; and her expression clouded, as though she had become aware of a barrier that sometimes exists between herself and other people.

[13-8] We both had difficulty understanding each other's speech. Imprecise pronunciation is a result of his auditory reception problems.

[14-6] He had difficulty understanding what is said rapidly, but understands the same words, said more slowly. It took me some time to realize this, because he does not talk slowly, he just *listens* slowly. This makes him seem less intelligent than he is.

Suggestion of Serious Difficulties in Language and Communication

Some language behaviors suggest serious problems:

[14-1] Sentence length and complexity (9-word sentence with a phrase or a clause) are on a kindergarten level, but conversational skills even on this level are lacking. Verbalization, even of personal questions, is entirely egocentric.

This shows grossly deficient language and social development.

[5-11] Conversation has an oblique quality. He answers Question #1 inadequately, then responds to Question #2 with the answer to Question #1. This suggests a time-lag in dealing with verbal material in conversation. He does not show this time-lag on structured tasks. He makes up words, which he can explain well when asked. Making up words is characteristic of younger children acquiring skills by playing with language, but his language is advanced far beyond this stage.

The child with this unusual receptive and expressive behavior had many other behavioral aberrations. His condition, once considered emotional, is now considered constitutional and treated with non-stigmatizing efforts to change target behaviors.

[10-6] He showed the following communication characteristics: (a) rambling, (b) getting derailed by his own thoughts, (c) a disordered relationship between the general and the specific (inappropriate overconcreteness and overgeneralization), (d) causal explanations that don't make sense, and (e) an odd flavor to his responses, including self-reference and implications of hidden symbolic meanings.

These are characteristics of a serious chronic emotional disorder believed to have a neurological basis.

Social and Cultural Factors

The cultural aspects of language involve subtle factors that can mislead people who think they speak the same language.

[14-9] He values a laconic style, which lowers his functioning on the test by imposing undue constraints: The one-word definitions he favors do not permit success on his level.

[18-3] She was self-conscious when giving a good verbal response, as though she did not consider it quite appropriate for her.

These illustrate the difference between lower socioeconomic and middle-class language values and its potential effect on school achievement. These students actually prefer the kind of language that teachers and test-makers consider inferior and resist school-like language as wordy and pretentious.

[17-5, English her second language] Her English is excellent in conversation, but she needs vocabulary-building to handle advanced academic concepts.

This bilingual newcomer to the country is at a middle stage of English acquisition that could easily mislead people into making greater academic demands than she is ready to handle.

A 10-year-old African-American girl, who had recently moved with her family from Mississippi to Chicago during the great migration, was given the current edition of the Stanford-Binet, which included an item about the similarity among several sets of three things. One set were all members of the vegetable kingdom. She answered that *they all put out vines*.

This was a very unusual answer. Wrong answers were almost always concrete descriptions of the three things separately (an apple you can eat, a daisy you can pick, and a tree you can climb).

The examiner asked what she meant by *vines*. She said that vines are *long things that grow out into the earth,* showing that she was expressing a correct answer, an age-appropriate verbal abstraction, in a different vocabulary, whether personal or regional-cultural.

Her response raised a question in the examiner's mind about how many other verbal misunderstandings had affected her scores.

A regional-cultural difference in word use came close to concealing this girl's abstract ability — and shows how language can be a mine field of misunderstandings.

[14-9] He is very conscious of language, and perceived regional cultural differences as language differences. This echoes his father's definition, as a French-Canadian, of ethnicity as language.

This perfectly bilingual family's language sensitivity had little bearing on the referral question, but brings a different perspective to the examiner-student duo: It is the examiner, who knows only English, who is culturally deprived.

Free Samples

There are times when only a direct quotation shows just how fractured language can be.

[6-3] "There was a acid-nets on the road, and they hadda blocks the road and it was all smashed up, all, all of it. The mirra smashed, [something about an] amulets. I think somebody got hurt."

[7-2] "They help the customers when something, when anything, or anything knocks down or something, they can fix something, cause they got parts to it and they got a lotta parts to it and they just give it back." "I make things you sorta something don't know mostly."

[12-10] *Hieroglyphics* are "stuff Egypts wrote on their walls." At 31,000 feet, "the air gets shorter."

These tidbits allow the speech/language specialist to decide whether to become involved in the case, and help explain written expression problems by showing that the speakers would have a hard time knowing what to write.

Test Behavior

Behavior Outside the Learning Process

Behavior that is *not* intrinsically related to learning is relevant to learning evaluations in helping identify nonacademic factors that might influence learning.

[7-10] He took my hand going to the testing cubby. He was enthusiastic in the morning, but exhausted and discouraged after lunch, and may still need his nap. To hold his attention during the Memory for Stories item [Stanford-Binet: L-M], I let him hold onto my hands. This had a beneficial effect.

This boy's dependency suggests that he may need more nurturance and less independence than some children his age. The easy fatigue suggests adjustment of his schedule for a rest after lunch.

[7-5] She had a way of "throwing it away" by gratuitous self-imposed handicapping, like not looking at a stimulus for the full exposure time on memory tasks.

This girl needs to learn *how* to learn, but even more, that her performance really does matter.

[10-7] She was very mature in social knowledgeability and competence, and shyly proud of these accomplishments. She is a better informant about her life than many adults, and is ready to assume responsibility for herself.

This student's realism and maturity could bring success in school and community activities, which might in turn encourage academic efforts.

[11-2] There was considerable difference in his appearance and performance between the two sessions. The first day he was bright eyed, well focused, and well organized. The second, he seemed preoccupied and did not tune in well.

This suggests that out-of-school events might be troubling this boy a great deal more on some days than others.

[14-10] She sometimes disobeyed trifling directions (*Point with the eraser, not the point, so you don't mark the book*). One response suggested that she still sees laws of nature as reflections of human authority. (When told to make the next block design using all nine blocks, she said in an irritated voice, "Do I *have to* use all nine blocks?"). Other responses suggested lingering dependency needs.

Subtle authority problems pervade this girl's thinking. Her teachers might be aware of this, allow some independence, and be tactful and supportive in making corrections. Having a teacher as a mentor might give her a more positive image of authority.

Learning-Related Test Behavior

The most important behavior in learning evaluations is behavior that is intrinsically learning related, because it shows how the person thinks and copes with learning tasks.

[10-11] Upon hearing, "I have nine cards with designs on them, etc." [Bender Gestalt], he immediately drew four lines dividing the page into nine spaces to contain, organize, and separate them.

This student is very quick to organize space for himself with guidelines and to know how best to divide a page into nine parts. Look for some adequate ability scores to match this show of competence. Look also for spatial problems he might be compensating for, and whether his compensation is successful.

[8-10] She used her verbal skills to talk her way through visual problems. She repeated to herself the names of the bead colors on the Bead Memory subtest of the Stanford-Binet: 4th edition. She used naming as a mastery technique (gave one face of the patterned blocks on the Pattern Analysis subtest the descriptive name, "bow").

This child depends to a great extent on verbal techniques to help her with visual tasks. See whether any scores or behavior show perceptual difficulties she is compensating for, or whether this is simply the preference of a child who enjoys language.

[13-0] He arranged all the Picture Arrangement items entirely in the left half of the work space.

In a person with academic difficulties, this behavior is fairly indicative of a learning disability. A 13-year-old who does not cross the midline merits consultation from the nearest occupational therapist.

[9-2] She tries to use her skills efficiently and reason things out. However, she does not have internal standards for achievement, and therefore is not sure how closely her work should approximate a model. When there is much detail, she does not integrate all of it, but works fast and impulsively.

One suspects this behavior is the effect of a nonacademic, nonachieving home environment. Instruction in problem solving — setting goals and working toward them step-by-step — is not a sure cure, but aims at the source of the difficulty.

[14-3] As an example of his brightness and abstract ability: I explained that because he moves and thinks so fast, he relies on hunches, and has never learned to think systematically. After I explained *systematically,* he drew the analogy to sounding-out words phonetically instead of sight-reading them.

Many very bright people share the problem of not having learned to work methodically, and one day schoolwork becomes too difficult for intuition alone. Past and present IQ scores would shed an interesting light on this behavior. This student has an additional problem. He is in a special class for behavior disorders where most students have learning problems. The academic work and instructional staff are geared to students far below his level. The result is loss of interest and self-esteem.

The Whole Description

No description in a report includes all the kinds of behavior illustrated above; the examiner selects some behaviors to record. These become more meaningful when they are combined into the whole description.

[7-11] He is a cute little boy with a small frame, large head, big eyes, regular features, and a mouth often slightly open. He is a gentle soul who is puzzled and frustrated by the physical world, and poorly oriented to both space and his own body. At one point, he nearly fell off his chair, and he seemed unable to cope with Kleenex. He sees the world as full of mysteries, secrets, and worries. In response, he either gives up, or tries so hard to please that he crosses himself up. I was sometimes able to help him succeed by telling him not to try so hard. He is a verbalistic child, who uses some very adult phrases to cover his inadequacies, without the understanding they imply ("I got a problem here," "I don't know, really. I'll try to think"), and generally feels he has to pretend to understand things he does not understand.

He has so much difficulty with visual space that it is hard for him to take a printed test. He does not know which hand is the right or the left one and cannot tell which is his dominant hand. He has difficulty placing the number in writing sums.

The physical description makes this boy seem frail and vulnerable. His open mouth suggests difficulties with either coordination or breathing. Behavior outside learning — inability to sit on a chair or blow his nose—supports coordination problems, although trying to blow his nose raises the possibility that he had a cold and was breathing through his mouth. (The examiner, who blows her nose often, ignored this.) Observers infer states of mind, like puzzlement and worry, from behavior. His response (giving up or trying too hard) to this subjective distress shows inability to cope effectively with his difficulties. His response to the examiner's intervention shows that he can benefit from direct instruction and suggests that his teacher could help him the same way in class.

Verbalism, visual–spatial difficulties, and handedness problems are learning-related test behavior. They fit well with the earliest-known kind of learning disability, a disability in visual and motor skills. Behavior outside learning—gross motor problems, and his puzzlement and frustration—also fits this pattern. His higher verbal skills and the endearing personal qualities seen in his appearance and behavior (gentle, follows instructions, uses adult phrases) provide some adaptive resources.

Before any test scores are reported, this boy has given the impression of a specific learning disability pattern. Final conclusions cannot be drawn without the scores, but the behavior described suggests a strong likelihood.

[11-11] He is a tall, thin, strong-looking boy, who appears already adolescent. He related in a mature, respectful way, and is easy to talk and work with. He grimaces when attempting something difficult, in a way associated with lack of differentiation of facial muscle movements, rather than a particular facial expression. He showed two behaviors characteristic of students who have endured much school frustration: (a) direct expression of frustration (muttering, "Oh, no!"), and (b) a studied look pretending he is trying hard to think of the answer, when he has actually given up. He told of his area of competence, working with tools. This is consistent with (a) some of his subtest scatter, (b) use of both hands alternately in pointing, and (c) excellent spacing of his Bender designs.

He has difficulty getting the big picture. He gets lost in specifics and has particular trouble seeing the relationship of the detail to the whole. This affects all his work, but especially inferential reading.

Appearance and relating described are positive: He is physically well-developed and conforming. Grimacing behavior represents a less mature global response instead of a more mature differentiated response. It is found in some younger children who require occupational therapy and, in a physically well-developed person, suggests unevenness among some of the components of sensorimotor integration. The school frustration behaviors tell that school has been hard for him: The first is a dramatized admission, the second an attempted cover-up.

His expressed liking for working with tools is learning related in that it shows a learning preference for the real world of mechanics outside school. At this point the description turns to subtest scores for support. The scatter mentioned consists of some significant subtest pair differences on the Stanford-Binet IV: In the Abstract/Visual Reasoning Area, he was higher in Pattern Analysis (similar to Wechsler's Block Design) and Matrices (abstract thinking on a visual task) than in Copying (designs in pencil); and in the Short-Term Memory Area, he recalled pictures of concrete objects better than linear arrangements of different-shaped beads or spoken number series. The weaker of these subtests have more in common with schoolwork, and the stronger more in common with mechanical tasks. Alternating hands suggests an ambidextrous tendency that sometimes accompanies school difficulties with good mechanical skills. Excellent use of space also fits in with mechanical ability.

This description does not list the details that went into the generalization that he has difficulty getting the big picture. This generalization is apparently based on a number of instances, which include behavior on the inferential reading test. The subtest strengths in Pattern Analysis and Matrices show that he *is* able to get the big picture on performance tests. His concreteness is in ideas.

This is a classic description of a boy who is "good with his hands but not good in school." Whether he is language learning disabled or a slow learner remains for the scores to show. Difficulty getting ideas points toward slow learner.

As manhood approaches, he is beginning to chafe (dramatizing, covering up) under the indignity of school failure. His mechanical ability might prove an outlet and a source of pride.

*   *   *

All these descriptive statements have been given to demonstrate the many-sidedness and range of behavior, even within the limited sample provided in the testing session.

3 THE INFLUENCE OF CONTRADICTION BETWEEN TEST SCORES, AND TEST BEHAVIOR AND OTHER INFORMATION, ON EXAMINATION CONCLUSIONS: A STUDY

Chapter 1 shows how test scores can sometimes lead to conclusions opposite from those drawn from test behavior and other information collected in a learning evaluation — background information, previous tests, and achievements.[1] Jason's WISC-R profile does not suggest learning disabilities, but his behavior does; and his achievements, which are significantly below his ability, round out the LD picture. His IQ score is average, but his behavior suggests above-average ability — supported by the previous test, which scored in the superior range before cumulative school difficulties lowered the results.

The question arises whether Jason is unique in this contradiction — an exception to the rules of test interpretation — or whether there is an appreciable proportion of cases like his. How much of the time are the interpretive implications of scores alone misleading?

To approach this question, I investigated a sizable sample of test reports that use the individualized level of interpretation. It is not easy to find such a sample. Most school examiners in my experience currently interpret scores alone.

General historical reasons for this state of affairs are discussed in the Introduction. For individual examiners, scores alone are simpler and easier to deal with, and professional training tends to be score oriented.

Two major textbooks on test interpretation (Kaufman, 1979; Sattler, 1988) both discuss the importance of behavior in test interpretation. But this message is easily missed. The space devoted to behavior is dwarfed by the space devoted to profile analysis. Pages of impressive statistical and other kinds of tables appear able to do practitioners' thinking for them, and do it right. Few of the sample case reports show the separate contribution of behavior to conclusions, or contradictory messages from behavior and scores.

Sattler and Kaufman also both introduce the notion of *hypothesis*. A hypothesis is an informed guess made on the basis of incomplete information. (All clinical examinations give incomplete information because they deal with samples of behavior.) Both books present the idea of *alternative hypotheses,* that an examination can give rise to more than one possible interpretation (Kaufman, 1979, pp. 14-18; Sattler, 1988, pp. 532-539). But the concept of alternative hypotheses should have been introduced before professional training, in the undergraduate general education science requirement, and reinforced by application to other subjects. Many examiners have missed out on this. If the reader has not already met alternative hypotheses, they are not likely to stick when first presented among more tangible bread-and-butter psychometric issues.

Therefore many readers of these authoritative and comprehensive textbooks overlook the sections on behavior and hypothesis-generation, and come away with the misconception that not only are scores the only data to interpret, but that in doing so, they are following Sattler and Kaufman.

Because of the prevalence of the mechanical level of interpretation, it is difficult to find a large number of individually interpreted reports to investigate, especially with the additional requirement of habitual description of learning-related test behavior. Therefore the sample consists of 295 of my own reports written over 4½ years. In many studies the sample is chosen for relative accessibility. This sample was uniquely accessible.

Some might criticize as circular the use of my own reports in an investigation of my recommended method of interpretation. These are not, however, presented as a standard of validity. They are presented as a sample of the universe of individualized test interpretation. Although I have not sampled this universe systematically, and do not know how representative these reports are, they are part of that universe. It is like studying one member of any group without knowing how typical that member is. The reminiscences of one Abenaki Indian, even an atypical one, tell something about the Abenaki culture, but must be interpreted with care. This is an investigation of the reports of one examiner who does individualized interpretation. It shows something about the method used in the universe of which they are a part, even though frequency statements can only be generalized with great care.

HOW THE EFFECT OF CONTRADICTION BETWEEN SCORES AND OTHER INFORMATION WAS STUDIED

Areas of Consistency vs. Contradiction

In order to study systematically the relative influence of scores as opposed to other information on examination conclusions, it was necessary to separate *areas* of possible contradiction. Four areas of diagnostic judgment were selected that include much of the potential contradiction and refer to readily available scores or measures.

Validity

The examiner must always make a judgment as to whether the test results are valid. The validity of all the scores can be seriously compromised by test-taking *set, conditions,* or *behavior.*

An example of a negative test-taking set is *lack of test motivation —* the attitude that testing is an unimportant activity and that it does not matter in the slightest whether one answers correctly, or performs rapidly when being timed.

An example of a negative test-taking condition is the situation in which examiner and subject were forced to move to a different room three times during the session.

An example of behavior that might negate test validity is *inability to focus* or *maintain attention* on the tasks given.

There is not always a clear line between set, condition, and behavior; but the distinction drives home the point that validity can be threatened by latent as well as overt behavior and by others' actions as well as the subject's.

There are many cases of attentional difficulty. Example 3-1 is one that called the test scores into question.

Other kinds of information contributing to judgments about test validity are outlined on pp. 56-57.

Qualitative Impression of Intelligence

The examiner's qualitative impression of the subject's intelligence is sometimes at variance with the IQ score. Although at one time the

---

Example 3-1

[Age 6-9, Kindergarten. School entrance was delayed one year when the kindergarten screening test showed "immaturity and potential school problems." Stanford-Binet, 4th edition Test Composite (equivalent to IQ) 74]

He did not focus his attention on test tasks without extra reminders. This difficulty affected many subtests and items. When he did manage to focus, however, something seemed to "click."

The effect of his focusing difficulty on test performance was so far-reaching that this behavior alone cast doubt on the IQ score as a firm prediction of ability.

IQ was considered sacrosanct (see, for example, Meehl, 1973, p. 241), the scientific climate has eased to the extent that a behaviorally well-documented qualification is now taken seriously. In order to make such a qualifying statement, the examiner should be able to convince a moderately skeptical reader — say a clinical instructor. There must be evidence for the judgment. The reason must be more than the subject's attractiveness, or the examiner's squeamishness or lack of self-confidence. An examiner should know better than both the educated layperson's misconceptions that IQ is the measure of true individual worth and an IQ below 90 or 110 is a misfortune, and the trainee's misconception that a normal IQ is the sign of an examiner's ability to build rapport.

There is ample general ground for qualifying the IQ scores of learning-disabled children. Learning disabilities lower IQ scores through both specific subscore weaknesses and more general conditions that affect the entire test. This is the reason learning-disabled populations have a lower average IQ than unselected populations. (See Stanovich, 1986, pp. 105-106.) But there must be evidence of higher individual ability beyond the existence of a learning disability. The same is true for other conditions that lower IQ scores, like emotional problems and cultural factors.

Judgments about whether behavior is consistent with IQ classifications rest on assumptions about what kind of behavior is characteristic of the standard IQ brackets (Average, Low Average, Superior, etc.). Behaviors used to delineate IQ classifications for the sample are outlined below (pp. 57-58).

The following excerpts show examples of behavior *consistent* and *contradictory* to general conceptions of the subjects' IQ classifications. Both subjects scored in the Low Average range. The first shows *consistent* behavior, that might be expected to accompany low-average ability — intellectual passivity, and difficulty with higher-order cognition.

Example 3-2

[14-9, WISC-R VSIQ 82, PSIQ 87, FSIQ 84] She is a quiet, subdued-looking teen-age girl. . . . She had a somewhat reproachful expression, interpreted as caused by the real difficulty of the material presented. Her approach to the work given was careful and methodical. She is not a language-oriented person. She had some difficulty comprehending oral language and orally presented problems, and she preferred making gestures to responding orally when there was a reasonable choice. She is not one to delve for verbal reasons and meanings. She demonstrated the same tendency her teacher mentioned, of trying to divine the answer from the examiner's response.

She expressed perplexity with other than social aspects of high school. In junior high she liked the individual explanations her teachers gave; but at high school, when she went for math help once, she was turned off by use of "long math words, like *quotient*.". . . . .

Summary: She tests in the low average, or slow-learner range of school ability.

The second subject shows *contradictory* behavior, that might *not* be expected with low average ability, but rather average and up — an active learner with a stock of academic coping skills.

Example 3-3

[10-6, Stanford-Binet IV, Verbal Reasoning Area 99, Abstract/Visual Reasoning Area 74, Quantitative Reasoning Area 82, Short-Term Memory Area 86, Test Composite 83] This boy, nearing the end of latency, was notable for his ability to cope with the total world of school. He is an excellent interview subject, who, to compensate for his auditory problem, takes a minute to think, and structures his response by asking for categories. He also provided his own structure

(continued)

Example 3-3 *(continued)*

when writing, by drawing the lines he needs. He understood the relationship between evaluation and services — creditable at any age — and made a reasonable request: a trial period without resource room help.

Summary: It would not be accurate to describe someone with these coping skills as a slow-learner. It would be more appropriate to say that his academic expectancy for some kinds of schoolwork is somewhat below his age level as a result of a combination of visual and auditory difficulties. . . . Tractability and motivation are positive factors.

Language Learning Disability

The most common kind of learning disability is language learning disability. (See Stanovich, 1986, pp. 110-111.) One attraction contributing to the popularity of the Wechsler tests is the Verbal–Performance discrepancy, which is associated with language learning disability. Not only is a Performance score significantly higher than Verbal often taken at face value as a sure sign of learning disability, but lack of this discrepancy is taken to mean the absence of learning disability. Yet language behavior and other information are also evidence, and sometimes confirm and sometimes contradict the implication of the Verbal–Performance discrepancy alone.

The following excerpts show examples of behavior *consistent* and *contradictory* to the Verbal–Performance discrepancy:

The first subject has the requisite discrepancy, and also shows behavior *consistent* with a language learning disability.

Example 3-4

[13-10, WISC-R VSIQ 74, PSIQ 112, FSIQ 91] His language difficulties include difficulty expressing himself orally and retrieving words. He has a flexible, field-independent approach to hand–eye tasks, with excellent motivation and concentration.

Summary: He is a language learning–disabled student. . . .

The following subject also has the discrepancy associated with language deficits, but his behavior *contradicts* the scores by demonstrating verbal ability and suggesting subtle attitudinal reasons for the relatively poor verbal test showing.

Example 3-5

[14-1, WISC-R VSIQ 84, PSIQ 102, FSIQ 91; significant strengths, Digit Span, Block Design, Coding; significant weakness, Similarities] He was proud of his achievement and verbal cleverness, announcing immediately, "I moved up, to algebra, from 'generic' math!" Yet he put little effort into testing because there was no direct reward (grades), and became impulsive and careless in problem solving.

He was high in subtests of automatic and content-free skills, and relatively weaker dealing with meaningful content. Lack of effort is one factor. Another is his intentional misinterpretation of language to frustrate and control the speaker; for him language is a weapon rather than a means of communication and learning.

His Performance-Verbal discrepancy does not reflect a language learning disability, but rather his differential involvement. Nor is he weak in verbal abstraction.

The next subject has a discrepancy that does not meet the standard for significance recommended in Kaufman's Practitioners' Rules (Chapter 1, p. 9). Behavior, however, nudges the conclusion toward language learning disability. This kind of contradiction shows that a discrepancy that is not significant can sometimes still be meaningful.

Example 3-6

[11-4, WISC-R, VSIQ 86, PSIQ 95, FSIQ 89] His attitude differed between language and spatial tasks. He resisted somewhat when asked for explanations and sometimes failed verbal items that seemed well within his scope; but on spatial tasks he responded rapidly, was serious and well-organized, and took responsibility.

Summary: Although the difference between his Verbal and Performance scores does not reach the level of statistical significance, his behavior is consistent with a language learning disability.

Other examples of discrepancies that are meaningful, although not significant by Kaufman's rule, appear in Jason's case, which is presented in full in Chapter 4, pp. 133-136; and Example 4-2, Chapter 4, pp. 86-88.

Other Learning Disabilities

Other kinds of learning disability (than language) are often associated with significant weaknesses of separate subtests and *factors* consisting of combinations of subtests. The best known of these factors is Freedom from Distractibility (Cohen, 1952, 1957, 1959) on the Wechsler tests, often called simply the Third Factor (Kaufman, 1979, pp. 74-76), consisting of Arithmetic, Digit Span, and Coding, as distinguished from the more language-oriented verbal subtests and the more simultaneous performance subtests. There are a number of other sets of Wechsler factors in use. Probably the second most influential is from Bannatyne (1971). Kaufman (1979, pp. 134-171) summarizes a great deal of the thinking and research about factors.

This investigation focused on subtest weakness and passed over factors. Computing factors for the 295 reports was just too laborious for the return. The most widely used, the Third Factor, makes an appearance in Chapter 5, where the diagnostic problem of attention deficit is represented by the cases of Ricky and Todd (pp. 154-161).

Example 3-7 describes a student whose test behavior is *consistent* with subtest weakness. In this example, the score, along with the test behavior, solves a long-standing diagnostic problem.

Example 3-7

George, 12-6, grade 6, is that existing rarity, a good student who has trouble with math and only math. One of the difficulties diagnosing such a student is that he does not test very badly in math compared to the referred population; but *he* knows, and his math teacher knows. Across-the-board tracking (homogeneous ability grouping) accentuates his problem: All his classes are for average and above-average students only.

A previous examination, age 8-11, grade 2, found WISC-R VSIQ 120, PSIQ 106, FSIQ 116, "numerical reasoning and concentration weak, careless, impulsive." Reading and spelling scores were above grade level, math at grade level. Yet the problem resurfaced.

The present examination found Kaufman Assessment Battery for Children Sequential Processing 93, Simultaneous Processing 108

(continued)

Example 3-7 *(continued)*

(a significant discrepancy); significant strength Photo Series, and *significant weakness Matrix Analogies.* Reading and spelling are still slightly, not significantly, above grade level. The Verbal and Quantitative Reasoning Areas of the Stanford-Binet, 4th Edition, were given to supplement the K-ABC. Verbal Reasoning was 115 and Quantitative Reasoning 88, a significant difference.

Particular attention was paid to George's behavior involving use of numbers.

1. Used cardinal numbers (*10, 16*) in writing sample.

   George understands whole numbers on a concrete level. He uses them as part of his life, including solving problems.

2. Used ordinal numbers ("This one's first . . . [through] this one's seventh") on K-ABC Photo Series (similar to Wechsler Picture Arrangement).

3. Counted the books in the bookcase to determine the time sequence on a Photo Series item.

4. Succeeded on many [S-B IV] arithmetic problems accompanied by picture illustrations.

   He is able to do math with concrete visual representation.

5. Had difficulty thinking of his age and his brother's age; knew his father's age (offered gratuitously, of course).

   This is unusual for a young person, and raises a question about whether he has failed to make some of the usual associations to numbers.

6. Counting the pieces in a picture of a pie, counted the first piece over at the end.

   This raises a question about the solidity of the basic counting process. It suggests the previous examination's "impulsive numerical reasoning." It could also reflect learned helplessness (Seligman, 1975) confronting math.

(continued)

Example 3-7 *(continued)*

7. In writing sample, wrote, "I have 10 or 16 of them."

This is an unusual usage. Since 10 and 16 are not close if the total number is in that vicinity, it suggests difficulty either sequencing or estimating.

8. Did not understand the meaning of the term *whole number.*

Many students this age do not understand these concepts, but a student with George's verbal ability might be expected to grasp some of them.

9. Did not understand the question, "What is the smallest whole number that can be divided evenly by __, __, and __?"

10. Did not understand $7 \div 1 = 7$.

11. Did not understand, "Which picture shows half as many _____ as _____?" (Chose the picture with an equal number of both.)

George's verbal skills are above average, his spatial skills are adequate, and his academic motivation is good. The K-ABC pinpoints a separate ability not sampled by his previous test. Even though it is presented visually, the Matrix Analogies subtest is *pure abstraction* which is neither verbal nor spatial. (Wechsler's Block Design has been equated with "nonverbal abstraction," but it is a spatial skill, "abstract" only in the sense of nonrepresentational, rather than pure abstraction—abstract art rather than abstract thought.) Pure abstraction deals with *relationships* as distinct from the things that are related. Mathematics is one of the few pure abstractions encountered in everyday life. (Genealogical relationships are another, but they have a ready-made visual aid, the family tree chart.)

George's Matrix Analogies subtest weakness, his gaps in math skills when assessed by curriculum samples, and the math behaviors described, all point to a learning difficulty specifically affecting math. His

(continued)

Example 3-7 *(continued)*

discomfort, in view of his relatively adequate math scores on norm-referenced tests, can be understood in terms of George's differing self-expectations from most referred students. He is not content to do math mechanically and squeak by, because in other subjects he achieves understanding and mastery.

Behavior that *contradicts* significant subtest weakness is seen in Example 3-5 (p. 51). The student has a significantly weak Wechsler Similarities subtest score, which is usually interpreted as verbal abstraction; but his comment, "I moved up, to algebra, from 'generic' math!" doubly contradicts any such weakness. Hanging a disparaging joke on the similarity of the words *general* and *generic* certainly shows abstract verbal ability. So does the fact that general math was too easy, and he was moved up to the more abstract algebra. The reasons for his low Similarities score are, rather, lack of test motivation, impulsivity, and preference for using his abilities for hostile and competitive purposes.

Identification of Consistent and Contradictory Information in the Four Areas

One source of information that can be either consistent or contradictory to test scores is *other test scores.* These include parts of the self-same test, like subtests of the main test, as well as other tests given at the same examination—tests of modalities, achievements, even personality. Wechsler Coding might be compared with the Bender Gestalt for another gauge of pencil skills, or Wechsler Arithmetic with a math test to separate calculation from listening. Projective tests also have cognitive and perceptual sides. Other specialists' tests contribute information. On re-evaluations, previous test scores show steady progress, forward leaps, or regression.

But much information is *descriptive,* words not numbers. In order to make uniform judgments about the consistency or contradiction with scores of a large number of descriptive statements, whose variety is only sampled in Chapter 2, one needs relatively clear-cut and objective grounds for comparing descriptions with scores—words with numbers.

I began by finding in the test reports *key phrases* related to the areas studied. In the area of **validity**, some of the consistent phrases, that tend to support test validity, were *able to sustain attention, well-intentioned,* and *self-motivated.* Some of the contradictory phrases, that might possibly cast doubt on test validity, were *preoccupied with inner concerns, resisted direction,* and *values speed at the expense of accuracy.*

To limit the number of different phrases while preserving their information, the phrases in each area were grouped in descriptive categories. Some of the categories under **validity** were *attention, cooperation,* and *motivation.* To simplify classifying phrases as consistent with scores or contradictory to scores, there were separate categories for each, so that *lack of attention, lack of cooperation,* and *lack of motivation* were categories as well. Once each phrase was categorized, the consistent/contradictory decision had already been made.

One of the descriptive categories consistent with scores, in the validity area, was *cooperation.* It includes such phrases as *obedient, well-intentioned,* and *easy to work with.* The corresponding category of contradictory information, *lack of cooperation,* includes *reluctant, resisted direction,* and *used delaying tactics,* among other phrases.

When students were described by both consistent and contradictory phrases in the same area (under **validity**, they might be *cooperative* and *motivated* but *unable to attend*), that area was classified as contradictory, because the contradictory behavior raised the shadow of doubt about the scores. When reports had neither consistent nor contradictory phrases in some areas, those areas were classified as consistent, because it was assumed that any reason for doubting the scores would have been stated.

Validity

Categories of information consistent with valid scores were: *attention, cooperation, motivation, good work habits, frustration tolerance, welcomes new experiences, positive personal qualities* (mature, stable, etc.), and *positive emotional state.*

Contradictory categories of information, that cast some doubt on scores, were: *lack of attention, lack of cooperation, lack of motivation, poor work habits, impulsivity* (when separate from *lack of attention*), *negative emotional state, difficulties resulting from handicapping conditions* (speech blocking, motor problems with cerebral palsy,[2] watching the examiner's mouth as if to "hear" better), and *other specific difficulties,* such as not working well under pressure, and self-imposed handicapping—the child who makes the task harder by setting additional constraints like doing Wechsler Coding without looking at the code key.

Unfavorable testing conditions were not mentioned, so apparently were not a problem in this sample.

Qualitative Impression of Intelligence

Spelling out the rationale for decisions about consistency vs. contradiction in this area forced me to face up to my implicit conceptions of different IQ levels. These were no less difficult to admit just because psychiatrists have been assigning intelligence levels for years without benefit of psychometrics ("This patient has low average intelligence"); and even proper examiners sometimes resort to such judgments off-duty.

These judgments, however, are not completely without basis. A list of the *behavioral indicators* used in the reports was developed. These are certainly not offered as complete or authoritative definitions, but merely to clarify one practitioner's working assumptions behind this study.

These indicators turned out to be coarser-grained than the classic IQ brackets. They mainly distinguished among average, above-average, and below-average, with an occasional foray into the superior and mental retardation ranges.

Some of the behavioral indicators span the whole intelligence range: *understanding either the immediate situation or life-in-general; quality of inferential or analytic reasoning; the concrete-to-abstract dimension of thinking; active versus passive problem solving; ability to learn in the immediate situation; compexity vs. simplicity of ideas; number and quality of associations; store of information about one's life,* relative to age; and *maturity*—developmental in young children, intellectual in older ones. Some of these wide-range indicators divide into different levels: On the concrete-to-abstract scale, *literal-minded* suggests below-average ability, *generalization* suggests average, and *abstract generalization* above-average. In active-to-passive problem-solving, *thinking things out* and *using strategies* suggest average ability. *Asking intelligent questions* and *questioning assumptions* suggest above-average. *Random perseverative efforts* suggests below-average. For associations, *paucity of content* suggests below-average ability; and *kid-literary references,* except for the most overworked and banal, suggest above-average.

The following characteristics draw the 90 IQ line—differentiate between below-average ability, and average-and-above: *flexibility versus rigidity of problem solving, divergent thinking* or *creativity,* and an *unusual store of knowledge* on a topic beyond the merely personal.

These signs suggest above-average ability: *multiple spontaneous responses; rapid but not impulsive responding; constructive curiosity,* to be distinguished from irrelevancies or distraction tactics; and *mature sense of social responsibility.* Sometimes *quality plus rapidity of reasoning* combine to produce a global impression of high ability.

Mental retardation is suggested by *social inappropriateness* that is naive rather than motivated or bizarre, and by *great difficulty retaining images of any kind.* Although the latter is also a sign of organicity, this degree of organicity can have a devastating effect on IQ. A group of varied specific behaviors suggest functioning above the retardation level, including *following complex directions, truly excellent attention and motivation,* and *intrinsic interest in academics.*

Other test information may call the IQ score into question: *scores indicating a higher level of ability on other parts of the same IQ test* that reflect higher-order cognition, or *other learning abilities tests;* on *achievements* (except spelling); in *adaptive behavior;* or on *projective test variables.* (One child's ability was actually judged lower than her IQ score from those last two plus her school history.) A *higher score on a previous examination* also often changes the picture.

Sometimes there are *detracting factors* that often lower IQ scores. Although positive evidence should be present before validity is challenged (see the caveat about learning disabilities on p. 48), examiners can be alerted to possible higher potential by *cultural deprivation* or *unusual background, learning disabilities, attention deficit, cumulative underachievement* (the learning-disabled student whose scores have slipped over time), *work habits* (*doesn't do well under pressure, holistic person* whose reversals lowered scores considerably), *specific handicaps* (the effect of language—lack of internal monologue—on problem-solving, or of fine-motor on performance tasks), or *emotional or other individual factors.*

Language Learning Disability

Study of this area was limited to students given one of the Wechsler tests.

Key phrases describing strong and weak receptive and expressive language behavior, like the examples on pp. 35-37, were compared with the presence or absence of the 12-or-more-point discrepancy in favor of Performance.

Other relevant test scores include Wechsler profiles that suggest language difficulties even though the classic discrepancy is absent, and evaluation by other specialists, especially in the language area.

Where the target judgment is a choice of one among several diagnostic categories (language learning disability, other learning disability, slow learner, within normal range), the *definition of the diagnostic category* sets requirements that serve as a final standard of consistency versus contradiction. Not only must a case fulfill the description, but it must also not be specifically excluded (". . . does not include students who have learning problems which are primarily the result of visual, hearing, or motor handicaps, of mental retardation, of emotional disturbance, or of environmental, cultural, or economic disadvantage." New Hampshire Department of Education, 1988, p. 3).

Other Learning Disabilities, Expressed in Subtest Weakness

Study of this area was limited to the Wechsler and the Kaufman Assessment Battery for Children, both of which have easily accessible or built-in criteria for significant subtest weakness. Significant subtest weakness was the score sign used as an indicator of learning disabilities.

Key phrases in the reports about the interpretation of the significantly weak subtests were compared with a standard interpretation. Standard interpretations of Wechsler subtests were defined more broadly than the formula used in Chapter 1, pp. 2-4, including such common practice as linking listening skills with the Information and Arithmetic subtests. Standard K-ABC interpretations followed the interpretive manual (Kaufman & Kaufman, 1983b, p. 205).

The Influence of Contradictory Information on Conclusions

Contradictory information can simply be *present* in a report without leading anywhere, and it can also *influence the conclusions*.

The reports were reviewed to find whether the conclusions of the examination were consistent or contradictory to the test scores in the four areas. The conclusions sought were not limited to those in the summary of the report, but sometimes appeared in the discussion instead, and occasionally even in a recommendation, like a request for consultation from the speech/language specialist for a child suspected of having a language learning disability.

THE FINDINGS OF THE STUDY

Classifying the other kinds of information in the reports besides the main-test scores as either consistent or contradictory to those scores made it possible to count the number of cases with consistent and contradictory areas. These, and the number of cases where contradictory information influenced the conclusions, are presented in Table 5. Findings are given for the areas of judgment separately and for the whole reports (unduplicated count).

Table 5 shows that the evidence from other information than main-test scores (i.e., behavior, other test scores) is rather evenly balanced between information supporting and information negating the thrust of the main-test scores, for both the separate areas and the whole reports. An unduplicated count shows considerable overlap among reports with consistent areas and those with contradictory areas: 127 (43.05%) contain both. An unduplicated count also shows that in

Table 5

Consistent and Contradictory Areas, and Influence of Contradiction on Conclusions

Area	N	Other information consistent with scores		Other information contradictory to scores		No relevant other information		Conclusions influenced by contradictory information	
		n	%	n	%	n	%	n	%
Validity	295	137	46.44	125	42.37	33	11.19	27	9.15
Qualitative impression of intelligence	295	41	13.90	49	16.61	205	69.49	37	12.54
Language learning disability	168	92	54.76	76	45.24	—	—	47	27.98
Other learning disabilities (subtest weakness)	213	68	31.93	70	32.86	75	35.21	70	32.86
Whole report (unduplicated count)	295	210	74.92	212	71.86	—	—	141	47.80

nearly half of all the reports, conclusions were influenced by contradictory information in one of the areas of judgment.

These proportions show that the examiner who undertakes individualized test interpretation has a great deal of information to consider in addition to the scores of the main test before reaching a conclusion.

Reasons for Contradictory Conclusions
in the Four Areas

Validity

The reason for concluding that the test scores as a whole were of doubtful validity usually appeared to be the degree of the negative behaviors rather than the specific behaviors. Attentional problems, which were common in the whole sample, figured in about half (14) of these cases and were often accompanied by other negative behaviors as well.

Qualitative Impression of Intelligence

The reason for questioning the IQ score was test behavior alone in 8 cases, other test scores alone in 5, and detracting factors alone in 1. In 15 cases it was some two of these combined, and in 8 cases all three.

The number of cases where contradictory information influenced conclusions about intelligence is probably minimal because of the influence on the examiner of bureaucratic regulations—eligibility requirements for getting help—and political pressures. (See Chapter 5.) These generally worked against expressed conclusions that the IQ may be higher than the score indicates.

When the purpose of testing is eligibility rather than understanding, the child's highest potential is not pertinent to that purpose and therefore tends to be left out, whether the district is restrictive or altruistic. In a district that required an IQ of 90 or above for learning disabilities services, as long as the IQ was 90 or above, there was no point saying it might be considerably higher. On the other hand, in a district that provided help for all who needed it, there was no need to mention higher potential.

In that more restrictive district, political pressures were common. Because the 90 IQ requirement for learning disabilities services was an economy measure, the administration did not welcome opinions that a student's potential was probably average despite an IQ score of 85. A subtler pressure was the condescending staff attitude toward the population of one school with many social and economic problems. Insisting that these people were really smarter than they appeared only invited a share of the scorn usually reserved for them.

Language Learning Disability

Contradictory cases in this area are nearly evenly divided between 26 false positives (the discrepancy without conclusions of language learning disability) and 21 false negatives (no significant discrepancy, but conclusions of language learning disability).

The most frequent (15) reason for false positives being judged *not* learning disabled was their achievements, which were judged adequate for the mainstream. Of the rest, 8 were more appropriately placed in other categories (4 had other kinds of learning disabilities, 2 were slow learners, and 2 emotionally handicapped). In 2 cases behavior negated learning problems, and 1 was attributed to educational deprivation through lack of attendance.

The reason so many students with a significant discrepancy had adequate achievements probably lies in the nature of the sample — 119 already coded, 93 of them learning disabled. Of the 15 false positives with adequate achievements, 9 were already coded learning disabled. The discrepancy shows the abiding psychological make-up of the language learning–disabled person, but their rehabilitation in special education had been successful. This does not mean that at this point they were discharged from their programs. The extent to which coded students remain coded is sometimes interpreted as showing the ineffectiveness of special education. It is rather the tendency of organizations to maintain the status quo apart from anyone's intention. If students' programs are successful, their parents want them to continue; if not, their teachers insist on it.

The reasons the false negatives *were* diagnosed language learning disabled were: 10 had visual or fine-motor in addition to language problems that smoothed down the discrepancy; 8 had behavioral indications of language problems; 2 had other indicative scores; and 1, whose discrepancy narrowly missed the criterion of significance, had formerly had an associated handicap.

Other Learning Disabilities

In this area of diagnostic judgment, *all* contradictory information influenced the conclusions. The reasons are the logical weakness of automatic subtest interpretations, which recognize far fewer causes affecting subtest scores than actually exist, and the statistical weakness of subtests, with their small samples of behavior and considerable test-retest variability.

In 13 of the cases where conclusions ran contradictory to a common interpretation of the scores, the subtest weakness nevertheless provided important diagnostic information. A weak Comprehension score often signaled difficulties with complex language, concepts, or higher-order cognition. Although these are not usually defined as learning disabilities, the subtest score is diagnostically useful combined with the behavioral evidence.

Contradictory conclusions in this area were all false positives — subtest weaknesses *not* interpreted as learning disabilities. (False negatives were not investigated. The task of identifying key phrases that contradict so large a number of normal scores would be formidable. A false negative normal Coding score might be identified by poor pencil skills on an achievement test of written expression, or on drawing tests like the Draw-A-Person and the Bender Gestalt; or poor sequencing skills, or poor visual memory for the Bender designs. Jason's report, Chapter 1, pp. 12-19, demonstrates false negative scores for a number of kinds of learning disabilities.)

As in language learning disability, a number (17) of the 70 false positives were *not* learning disabled because of adequate achievements. Of this 17, 10 were already coded learning disabled. A few of the false positives, again, belonged in other categories — slow learners, mental retardation. Some relatively weak scores were not absolutely weak at all.

Most (26) of the false positives, however, were caused by diagnostic reasoning. In 8 cases, the standard subtest interpretation was contradicted by other test information, like success on similar tasks or previous examinations. In 7 cases, the weakness shown by the subtest was not considered a learning disability, like low Information scores as a result of cumulative nonachievement. In 15 cases, the subtest scores were judged to have an individual meaning instead of the standard interpretation: K-ABC Hand Movements (imitating a series of gestures from memory) was lowered by initial anxiety, and Arithmetic by stopwatch anxiety. Comprehension was a complex language challenge to some, and Similarities and Arithmetic a convergent task challenge to another. Language difficulties obscured the meaning of the Picture Arrangement stories for some; another was too self-absorbed to be interested in them. Object Assembly showed problem-solving rigidity rather than visual or hand–eye skills. All the possible meanings of any subtest have not been completely catalogued.

IMPLICATIONS FOR THE ROLE OF THE EXAMINER

Much of the reasoning behind the contradictory conclusions involves integrating learning-related test behavior with a variety of scores. This changes the perception of the role of the examiner. No more pair-of-hands, whose product—the test scores—can be dissected by team members, consultants, and supervisors equipped with code books and software for translating subtests into learning classifications. The examiner is the only person who has access to the learning-related test behavior. The examiner may not necessarily have observed, recorded, understood, and interpreted the pertinent behavior, but the examiner is the only one in the position to do so.

4 THE PROCESS OF CLINICAL INFERENCE

This chapter describes the process of reasoning from the data[1] of a psychological examination to its conclusions.

The first part of the chapter discusses the logic of clinical inference. Logic is the bare-bones framework — the outline, the pattern, the form — that lies behind the reasoning about information in specific cases. This framework of reasoning is the same for all fields of knowledge, the so-called *hard* sciences — physical and biological sciences and experimental psychology — as well as clinical science.

The discussion emphasizes nonquantitative data, chiefly test behavior. Chapter 2 illustrated the many-sidedness and range of test behavior; and Chapter 3 showed that learning-related test behavior is an important part, along with test scores, of the information used in individualized test interpretation. There are already excellent books (for example, Kaufman, 1979, 1990; and Sattler, 1988) that give full treatment to reasoning about quantitative information. It is hoped that the present book, in emphasizing the other side, will round out the picture.

Some of the early examples of reasoning in this chapter are from life-in-general rather than clinical inference. Be patient. Examples from clinical inference will soon follow. Many clinical matters are so debatable that it is easier emotionally to see the form of reasoning on a neutral topic; and the use of certain classic logical examples helps tie clinical inference to reasoning in other fields. The natural starting-place, the simplest form of logic on which the rest is built, deals with statements that apply to everyone in a given group. Clinical examples are scarce to nonexistent, because in clinical science almost nothing is true of all the members of any category.

Some have interpreted this lack of universal rules to mean that clinical inference is not logical. If the present discussion tells more about logic than practitioners need to master, it does so in order to draw clinical inference into the circle of respectable scientific thought by showing that it *is* logical and follows the same rules of reasoning as all other fields of knowledge.

The second part of the chapter applies the logic described in the first part to a particular case, and a familiar one. This part proceeds in the natural order of the examiner's experience, first the problem, then the data, and then the reasoning process, including the subjective side of reasoning, the psycho-logical along with the logical.

The chapter ends with a view beyond question-and-answer, problem-and-solution, to the examiner's purpose apart from the daily demands of the job. For logic and reasoning are only methods, or means. The ends—the uses to which they are put—are the ultimate test of worth of problem solving. Valuable goals, however, can hardly be reached by faulty reasoning.

Part 1.
The Logic of Clinical Inference

Knowledge about data—particular events—does not have the same scientific or humanistic status as general knowledge—knowledge about classes of events. "My daughter lost a tooth on her sixth birthday" is gossip. It is trivial except to the child and her mother. But that *all children lose their teeth at about that age* is general knowledge of child development.

Knowledge of particular events is enhanced by knowledge of the relevant generalizations, as when knowledge of a daughter's lost tooth is grounded in the knowledge of the stage of development taking place, the understanding of the chain of events that has taken place and stretches into the chain of events to come. A tooth is no longer merely a tooth. Losing it becomes more important than the momentary pain, the surprise, the coin left under the pillow. This small temporary loss ushers in the prime school learning years of latency.

At the same time, general knowledge is of little use unless it is applied to particular situations. Scientific knowledge involves an interplay between general laws and specific events.

Clinical data are brought into the scientific fold the same way any particular events are connected to general knowledge: by being recognized as examples of general principles.

PATTERNS OF REASONING

There are three patterns of reasoning between the particular events and the general principle: the syllogism, induction, and association.

The Syllogism

There is an old and honored formal chain of reasoning between the particular and the general. It is called the syllogism.[2] The basic form of the syllogism is:

Major Premise:	All persons are mortal.
Minor Premise:	Hypatia is a person.
Conclusion:	Therefore Hypatia is mortal.

A syllogism is an arrangement of three nouns (or other words that name), which are called the *terms,* in three sentences. Each sentence links two different terms, round-robin. The major premise links a group or class, *persons* (the first term), with a predicate, *is mortal* (the middle term). The minor premise places an individual, *Hypatia* (the third term), within the class,[3] *persons.* The conclusion follows inexorably from the two premises in applying to the individual, *Hypatia,* the predicate of her class, *is mortal.*

Weaknesses and Solutions

As a means of attaining knowledge about individuals, the syllogism has several weaknesses:

Banality. The syllogism above is all very well and true, but it probably does not tell any more about Hypatia than we knew to begin with.

The inconsequential nature of the syllogism, however, is reversed by simply reversing the order of the two premises. Beginning with the minor premise, Hypatia's personhood, one can reason that all kinds of knowledge about persons apply to her, including that she was someone's daughter and probably lost a tooth at the age of 6. It is by such reasoning that fortune-tellers come up with their amazing insights.

Application of knowledge about child development to individual children follows the pattern of the reversed-premises syllogism.

Tiffany is 6 years old.
Six-year-olds are active, boisterous, challenging, dramatic, eager, exploratory, fearful, and indecisive (Gesell & Ilg, 1946, pp. 88-130).
Therefore Tiffany has these qualities.

Overgeneralization. A weakness of the reversed-premises syllogism is overgeneralization from placing the individual in too broad a class. Tiffany may not be typical of 6-year-olds in the respects listed. More careful reasoning is achieved by limiting Tiffany's class to a more manageable and predictable one than 6-year-olds.

Tiffany is a very small 6-year-old from the Pierce family.
Small 6-year-olds sometimes act more like 5-year-olds.
The Pierce children have all matured slowly in early childhood.
Therefore Tiffany might be expected to act more like a 5-year-old than a 6-year-old.

This time Tiffany is placed in two more limited and predictable classes: *small 6-year-olds,* and *Pierce children.*

The Fallacy of the Undistributed Middle, or Guilt by Association. Another weakness of syllogisms is that they are readily subverted into a form similar in appearance, but completely wrong:

All dogs are animals.
My cat is an animal.
Therefore my cat is a dog.

The error is a minor premise that links the individual case with the wrong term—the predicate (*animals*) instead of the class term. The predicate (*animals*) is much broader than the class (*all dogs*), for *animals* include many creatures besides dogs, so that something can be an animal without being a dog. The name *undistributed middle* means that the middle term, the predicate *animals,* is not applied exclusively ("distributed") to the class *all dogs.*

The error is easy to see with cats and dogs, but can be more difficult with emotionally charged terms.

Communists have beards.
The young man who has applied for the junior high school teaching position has a beard.
Therefore the young man who has applied for the junior high school teaching position is a communist.

Psychology claims its share of this fallacy:

Schizotypal personalities believe in clairvoyance.
Mrs. Sosostris believes in clairvoyance.
Therefore Mrs. Sosostris is a schizotypal personality.

People with cerebral lesions have difficulty copying designs on the
  Bender Gestalt.
Rasheed has difficulty copying designs on the Bender Gestalt.
Therefore Rasheed has cerebral lesions.

So does education:

All dyslexics read symbols backward.
Matthew, age 6, reads symbols backward.
Therefore Matthew, age 6, is a dyslexic.

Learning-disabled students have higher Performance than Verbal IQs.
Andy has a higher Performance than Verbal IQ.
Therefore Andy is learning disabled.

Syllogisms can only place individuals in categories of disorders
(*cerebral lesions, dyslexia, learning disabled*) if the disorder is the
predicate of the syllogism.

All persons who have a certain symptom have such-and-such a disorder.
Melissa has the symptom.
Therefore she has the disorder.

Not—

All persons with such-and-such a disorder have a certain symptom.
Melissa has the symptom.
Therefore she has the disorder.

The second syllogism is wrong because as the premises are stated, it
is perfectly possible to have that certain symptom, like *belief in clairvoyance,* and *difficulty copying Bender designs,* and *occasionally
reading symbols backward,* without having the disorder sometimes
associated with the symptom.

The difficulty with using the syllogism to place people in categories
is that hardly any signs always signify a given category, and hardly
any symptoms always signify a given disorder.

The solution is to have enough supporting evidence, and check for
possible contrary evidence, before categorizing individuals.

The Probable Predicate. The greatest drawback to use of the
syllogism in clinical inference is the scarcity of universally true

statements. The child development field appears to be chock-full of general statements about how and when children develop; however these statements are norms rather than universals. Fortune-tellers serve the general public, but clinicians tend to meet the exceptions. Tiffany, age 6 (see p. 68), may have the developmental age of a 5-year-old and have a different set of characteristics than the list given.

In psychology, almost the only universal statements about individuals have been those made on faith — assumptions, usually disproven or discredited a generation later, like "All aggression results from frustration," and "All psychological problems originate in the first 5 years of life (preferably the first 2)."

Most general statements about individuals are statistical, or *probabilistic*. They are statements about a proportion of the population. These statements are true about the whole population, but there is no way of knowing, on the face of it, whether they are true for any one individual. There is instead a *probability* that the statement is true for the individual.

A typical statement is, "Two-thirds of the learning-disabled persons have language problems."[4] Presumably they have a (significantly) higher Performance than Verbal IQ. Knowing that one-sixth of the general population has this discrepancy (Kaufman, 1976), and assuming the prevalence of learning disabilities in the population to be one-tenth,[5] by some calculation[6] we can formulate this syllogism:

> People with higher Performance than Verbal IQ have a 40% probability of being learning disabled.
> Andy has a higher Performance than Verbal IQ.
> Therefore Andy has a 40% probability of being learning disabled.

This is a perfectly good syllogism; but because the predicate is a probability, it still does not tell whether Andy is learning disabled.

There are two solutions to this quandary, two ways to tighten the net of probability around the individual case:

(1) **The Statistical Solution: Increasing the Numerical Probability.** If Andy has other characteristics, besides his Performance-Verbal discrepancy, each of which carries a probability of placing him in the learning-disabled category, the total probability would increase with each additional characteristic. Without gathering any more information about Andy, there is another fact already implied that adds to the odds of his having a learning disability: *he was referred.* This increases his chances over the general population, in addition to his test score discrepancy. Each separate strand increases the net additively.

(2) The Clinical Solution: Discovering the Internal Connection.[7]
Probability does not have to involve frequency. It can also use logical
evidence.[8] Such evidence might appear in Andy's achievements, his
learning-related test behavior, his developmental history. Achievements
notably below expectancy, inefficient and circuitous reception and
response to stimuli, and a positive history, all would support an internal
connection. These new strands, instead of being simply added, are
arranged in an interdependent pattern or configuration. We call the
perception of this configuration *understanding*.

These webs of events are often thought of as causal. The events in
the web can either exist at the same time (synchronous), or they can
exist in a sequence or time-line. As an example of the two kinds of
time relations in the pattern, take Jamie, who has been referred for
both learning and behavior problems.

The **synchronous web** involves the interaction of a number of factors,
none of which came first, or began at an identifiable time, but which
are inherent in Jamie and his entire situation, so that it would be
difficult to alter or remove any one of them. Jamie comes from a family
of persons, especially the males, who have had difficulty in school and
in society. He entered school, and probably was born, with a nervous
system which in some respects was not as developed as most children's.
The authority structure in his family is not as strong as his teachers
would like to see; but then, few of todays' families are the kind the
teachers consider optimal, including many of the teachers' own families.
The children's diet, like most children whose parents are not regarded
as zealots, is heavily weighted with sugar, and contains many artificial
colorings and chemical preservatives. Like most other children, Jamie
spends a great deal of time watching television. Television bombards
both senses at once, which does not encourage the development of
the separate senses (looking and listening); presents brief scenes which
encourage rapid shifts of attention; and features violence, and joking
denigration of women in a context that equates criticism with
humorlessness.

The **time-line** starts with the child, born with a certain heredity and
nervous equipment, and traces his development from this mildly
unready newborn. He begins to walk early, before he is able to sort
out stimuli or attend to his mother's admonitions. He darts rapidly
around the apartment, breaking things and endangering himself. His
mother becomes overwhelmed and angry. First she is physically
punitive. Soon she gives up, and lets him run wild; but the results of
her own child-rearing are so difficult to tolerate that she begins to go

out a great deal, leaving him with a succession of even less effectual
teen-age baby-sitters. Because of these developments, he is an impulse-
ridden child who has few inner controls and cannot accept outer
ones.

Think of the factors in the synchronous web as a handful of
jackstraws, all thrown at once, mutually interdependent, hard to
extricate one at a time. The time-line is a row of dominoes standing
on edge. One falls against the next, that one against the next, and so
on, until all have fallen.

The synchronous web tends to be morally neutral, as it is difficult
to assign blame on the basis of interlocking factors. The time-line tends
to assign blame, usually to the primary care-giver. The synchronous
web is roughly equivalent to Aristotle's *material* cause, the time-line
to his *efficient* cause.[9]

Induction

When people learn by their own experience, they discover particular
events before they discover general knowledge. General knowledge
is forged out of many repeated instances of similar particular events.
The form of reasoning that combines particular events into general
knowledge is **induction,** or inductive reasoning.

Its classic form is simple induction:

Monday morning the sun rose.
Tuesday morning the sun rose.
Wednesday morning the sun rose.
Thursday morning the sun rose.
Friday morning the sun rose.
Therefore every morning the sun rises.

The reverse phase of induction is **deduction,** or deductive reasoning, which begins with an established generalization and reasons to
a particular instance:

Every morning the sun rises.
Tomorrow is another morning.
Therefore tomorrow morning the sun will rise.

If this rings a bell, it is back to square one and the syllogism, with
its familiar strengths and weaknesses.

These two forms of reasoning are often combined in use into
inductive-deductive reasoning. In this form, the generalization is left
unsaid, and the events that led to it bring an immediate conclusion

about another similar event. The unspoken generalization is understood:

Monday morning the sun rose.
Tuesday morning the sun rose.
Wednesday morning the sun rose.
Thursday morning the sun rose.
Friday morning the sun rose.
Therefore tomorrow (Saturday) morning the sun will rise.

The Weakness and Its Solution

Inductive reasoning is not considered in itself proof positive, because the sample is never complete. No universal generalization constrains future events to conform to past ones. The successful completion of inductive reasoning is to be found, not in the repetition of instances, but in the same internal connection that solved the probability conundrum (pp. 71-72).

Take a case where the conclusion merits some doubt:

Monday morning Megan stood on the corner waiting for the bus.
Tuesday morning Megan stood on the corner waiting for the bus.
Wednesday morning Megan stood on the corner waiting for the bus.
Thursday morning Megan stood on the corner waiting for the bus.
Friday morning Megan stood on the corner waiting for the bus.

It is not inevitable that Saturday morning will find Megan on the corner waiting for the bus. She may be 10 years old, and may have been waiting for the school bus all week. If this is the case, she will not be there on Saturday. The internal connection refutes the conclusion.

Thus the real force of the sunrise argument is not the inductive form, but the internal connection of a celestial mechanism. Before the mechanism was known, the next day's sunrise was as tenuous as the comings and goings of neighbor Megan, and was cast into doubt by every winter solstice, every eclipse.

In order to reach a solid inductive conclusion, then, it is necessary to find an internal connection. Finding one can include thinking of a new one.

Inductive Reasoning in Clinical Inference

Induction is used in drawing conclusions from a number of behavior samples. This is an example from test interpretation:

Michelle read *M* for *W*.
Michelle read *b* for *d*.

> Michelle read *saw* for *was*.
> Michelle wrote her name from right to left.
> Michelle copied 6 of the 9 Bender designs sideways or upside-down.
> Therefore Michelle makes reversals.

An associated deduction might be

> Children who make reversals benefit from the Frostig materials.
> Michelle makes reversals.
> Therefore Michelle would benefit from the Frostig materials.

The inductive-deductive form would be

> Michelle read *M* for *W*, *b* for *d*, and *saw* for *was*; wrote her name from
> right to left, and copied 6 of the 9 Bender designs sideways or
> upside-down.
> Therefore Michelle would benefit from the Frostig materials.

Many acts of induction are based on a very small sample, sometimes even only one event. This is acceptable to the extent that the sample is an inseparably characteristic part of the whole. ("You don't have to eat the whole egg to know it's rotten.") Sometimes a small-sample induction is little more than a shift in phrasing from a particular observation to a generalized description (see pp. 113, 118-120):

> Reading and decoding errors show difficulty with one-syllable words
> and blends.
> Reading decoding is a serious problem for Jason, grade 4.

Other small-sample inductions involve more free-wheeling inference:

> On Vocabulary, Jason made associations to relevant facts easily and
> packed a great deal of relevant information into medium-length
> responses.
> On Vocabulary, he gave the impression of being very intelligent.

Although this inference might be said to contain a hidden major premise (people who respond this way are very intelligent), it is also a generalization, that as Jason acted on the Vocabulary subtest, he might also be expected to act the rest of the time.

Clinical inference also uses inductive-like reasoning to group together a number of events that are similar only because they are already classified together in the examiner's conception. They may be connected by a synchronous web or a time-line, or they may belong to a conception or definition of the same syndrome or disorder:

> Jamie does not sit still for more than 30 seconds.
> Jamie has difficulty attending to tasks.

James is easily distracted.
Jamie has difficulty waiting his turn.
Jamie does not finish what he starts.
Jamie plays boisterously.
Jamie talks non-stop.
Jamie does not listen to adults.
Therefore Jamie has many characteristics of attention-deficit hyperactivity disorder.
(Or, Therefore Jamie has attention-deficit hyperactivity disorder.)

An associated deduction would be

Children with attention-deficit hyperactivity disorder benefit from stimulant medication.
Jamie has attention-deficit hyperactivity disorder.
Therefore Jamie would benefit from stimulant medication.

The inductive-deductive form would be

Jamie does not sit still for more than 30 seconds, has difficulty attending to tasks, is easily distracted, has difficulty waiting his turn, does not finish what he starts, plays boisterously, talks non-stop, and does not listen to adults.
Therefore Jamie would benefit from stimulant medication.

Association

The view is commonly held (for example, see Wertheimer, 1945/1959, pp. 5-11), that thinking by association is quite separate from logical reasoning; that association is natural and undisciplined, whereas logic is artificial and rule-bound. People overlook their similar function in thinking. *Associational processes serve the same purpose as syllogisms and induction — linking the particular instance with the general class —* which is the essential feature of any practical art that employs scientific principles (general knowledge). The difference is that in association, the general class is not always identified.

Sometimes the practitioner is reminded by one person of another without knowing why, jumping from particular case to particular case without going through the generalization that connects them. Aaron is somehow reminiscent of Amy. His tip-toe walk suggests her stiff carriage of head and arms. His tangential conversation is somewhat like — and somewhat different from — her calling words out of the blue. The examiner does not know the connection and may not even be able to define the similarity.

When people think, "That reminds me of another case . . . ," they often do not recognize that general knowledge has a place in their thinking. But the similarity suggests that *the cases are alike because they belong to the same general class,* even though neither the similarity nor the class is named. *Similarity,* with its implication of classifying the world of experience, has been called a basic element of thought (Russell, 1940, pp. 344-347).

The drawback to association is that it can happen on the basis of incidental characteristics that are not necessarily relevant to the referral question, and may even be prejudicial. Examples are facets of appearance, and ethnicity. Therefore it is not safe to trust associations until the general class is identified, or at least until further evidence confirms a relevant similarity. Aaron and Amy might both have similar unusual early development patterns or respond to the same teaching methods. One's colleagues' independent agreement may confirm the objectivity of the perception of similarity, although it does not provide the missing link.

Association is not unscientific. It is a good beginning, but it is incomplete and unproven until there is some understanding of the nature of the general class. The class is the internal connection between Aaron and Amy.

HOW THE INTERNAL CONNECTION IS DISCOVERED

A number of theoreticians have come up with hypotheses about how the inductive leap to an internal connection occurs. A hypothesis is a well-informed guess. Most of these hypotheses do not stop with induction alone, but include the critical review that comes afterwards. Yet the act of discovery merits separate attention, because it is the heart of the clinical inference process, and because it is the part considered difficult, and is difficult to communicate about. It is a creative act, with the same relationship to the critical after-review that creative writing has to editing. Most people believe they can learn editing and critical review by a set of rules; but they are more doubtful about the possibility of attaining creation and insight. Therefore the inductive leap is discussed here before the critical after-review (*Proof in Clinical Inference,* pp. 80-82).

Models of Problem Solving

Saying that an inductive leap takes place is one thing; describing the process is another. Most attempts to describe it fall short of producing the very configurational understanding they seek to describe.

A Contemporary Model

Today's most popular model of problem solving is a *mechanical model*, which is applied to logical and mathematical problems like chess moves. The first preparatory step is to generate a list of all the possible solutions to the problem, which may run to millions. Next comes a mechanical search through all these solutions for the best fit, with a corresponding wait for the search of the databank.

Expert practitioners often prove superior to the mechanical model (Taylor, 1990). Their superiority appears to lie in their ability to *focus,* or *select* information most likely to be helpful, thereby cutting through large amounts of irrelevant material. (For a geometric analogy to this cutting-through process, see Gleick, 1984, on Karmarkar's algorithm.)

The "Ordinary Language" Position

Selective focus is the crux of the model offered by the "ordinary language" school of thought, an also-contemporary philosophic position. (See Austin, 1961.) This viewpoint holds that people think in prototypes, patterns that real objects and events approximate, stripped of extra details. The habit of thinking in configurational webs among prototypes certainly simplifies inference, but it tends to overlook individual characteristics. It also sharply decreases the possibility of making new discoveries.

Creative Problem Solving

A conceptualization of creative problem solving, influenced by gestalt psychology, was proposed by Graham Wallas (1926). It consists of four steps: *preparation, incubation, illumination,* and verification, which has more aptly been renamed *revision* (Johnson, 1955, p. 264). In clinical science, *preparation* is the gathering of evidence: records-reading, observation, interview, testing. *Incubation* is a period during which ostensibly nothing happens, and the problem-solving processes lie fallow; but some subliminal process apparently takes place, which results in a sometimes quite sudden *illumination*: the inductive leap to the solution, the perception of a new configuration, understanding. Gestalt psychologist Max Wertheimer (1945/1959) has written a fascinating book chronicling a number of instances of illumination in mathematical and spatial problems. *Revision* is the critical after-review, discussed below under *Proof in Clinical Inference* (pp. 80-82).

An Integration

In the description of the clinical problem-solving process offered here, the problem (referral question) sets the selective focus, which in turn shapes the information gathering. Next comes an attempt to link the information gathered, on one hand, with the problem (referral question) on the other, by a configurational web (explanation). The *linking* is a chain of associations. It consists of searching through all similar known *terms* (see *The Syllogism,* p. 67) and their associated explanatory webs, to see if any web includes both a problem-term and an information-term. Some of the terms may be prototypes, some not. A term need not be a word. It can be a look, gesture, odor, or feeling.

The process described so far is similar to the mechanical model. In some cases the solution will be found, and the search will end here.

When no answer has emerged, or the answer has not met the standards for justification and proof (see below, pp. 80-82), the situation calls for a switch from convergent to divergent thinking — from already-known, familiar answers, to individualized problem solving. The clinician must try another tack. This might be a change of emphasis or configuration, like de-emphasizing test scores in favor of behavior.

Another tack can also be a search for further information that might imply a new explanation. Then the selective focus of the initial search is to some extent reversed, and there are successive searches of broader and broader territory that might suggest new configurations. Review with an even sharper eye the information gathered about the child and the situation. See if there are gaps in the information — perhaps the classroom situation has not been sufficiently observed. Then call upon a broad background of information that has not been assumed to be directly related to the case. Perhaps the same teacher had a problem with a similar child 3 years ago; or the internal connection points to theories out of favor with one's colleagues like *strephosymbolia* (Orton, 1925, p. 610), or late blooming (Ilg & Ames, 1964/1972); or the learning style may characterize a low-frequency cultural group.

Sometimes time is on the opposing side. New information turns up after the deadline. One girl's inability to read was inconsistent with her test pattern. No other clues appeared until her family came to review the test findings, when unsuspected developments pointed to an emotional dimension. Sometimes it is necessary to talk to a colleague, go to the library, seek out a former professor. Sometimes the explanation is in the forefront of knowledge, or has not yet been discovered.

In conclusion, everything the examiner knows, has read, and can learn, both in the particular field of knowledge and outside, is data to access in search of an explanation. Otherwise solutions are limited to a comparatively narrow, canned list. All the solutions considered possible on one day do not exhaust the possibilities of another day.

DISCOVERY VS. PROOF

The traditional viewpoint in psychology has been that clinical investigation leads to *discovery,* but *proof* comes only through statistical methods, the computation of mathematical probability. This means the clinician cannot be certain of anything, because certain knowledge about individuals is impossible. The closest we can come to certainty is knowing the probability of scores within the band of error. A classic presentation of this view of discovery and proof appears in Meehl (1954).

Limiting oneself to statistical reasoning—scores alone, mechanical interpretation—in hopes of achieving greater certainty, however, also limits the usefulness of the examination.

Statistical proof addresses questions about *yes-no decision making,* whether there is an acceptable probability that a person falls on one side of a line or the other, in one category or another. Statistics does not deal in reasons—internal connections. In practical matters there are always particular circumstances to consider. Whatever the yes-no decision or the category, there remain questions about what to do about the matter day-to-day. Statistical proof cannot take into account circumstances that did not go into the original calculations, or answer day-to-day questions. Only discovery of the internal connection can do that.

Meehl (1958, pp. 500-503; 1973, pp. 250-252, and 259-261) gives examples of the conflict between statistical and clinical reasoning that are so affect-laden that they are difficult for many clinicians to accept even after all these years. A neutral nonclinical example is the one-lane railroad underpass located on a sharp dog-leg turn in the Winona Lake Road in New Hampton, New Hampshire. The local people claim there has never been an accident there. The police say this is an exaggeration, but there have been far fewer than might have been expected. According to statistics, the underpass is not dangerous; according to causal reasoning, it is. But they answer different questions. Statistics answers questions of numerical prediction—how many accidents to expect next month. Causal reasoning answers questions of action— how fast to drive, whether to put up warning signs. It is only because people have answered these practical questions sensibly in the past that accidents have not been more frequent.

Statistical reasoning also serves different social goals than causal reasoning. Statistical reasoning, which is about the population as a whole and is not concerned with extenuating circumstances for individuals, tends to be used when the good of society is valued over the good of individuals. It is efficient for reducing the number of undesired events—harm and waste. An example is preferring not to risk hiring unfit people as pilots or police officers, or wasting scarce resources like psychotherapy on poor candidates, at the risk of denying opportunity to some who could succeed. This was the prevailing mood in the 1950s. Causal reasoning is better suited to goals of extending opportunities to individuals even at some risk to society. An example is finding ways to provide job opportunities, special education, and psychotherapy to the neediest regardless of risk of failure, as is favored today.

The limitations of purely statistical reasoning about individuals have been recognized in a national trend that emphasizes descriptive definitions and standards at least as much as numerical ones, for mental retardation (Grossman, 1977), educationally handicapping conditions (New Hampshire Department of Education, 1988), and mental disorders (American Psychiatric Association, 1980, 1987).

There is a school of thought (see Note 8) that defines probability to include logical as well as statistical support (see *The Clinical Solution,* pp. 71-72). Including logical support opens the door to *proof of the internal connection.*

PROOF IN CLINICAL INFERENCE

Clinical inference is proved, for the time being, by showing that the explanation answers the question asked, and answers it better than alternative explanations. It is proved or disproved in the long run by whether or not subsequent events bear it out.

Cross-Checking the Evidence: The Criteria of a Theory

Bits and clusters of information suggest explanations. Such incomplete or tentative explanations are called *theories* or *hypotheses.* (A theory explains a more complex set of events than a hypothesis, and usually covers more than one case.) Sometimes some information points to one explanation, and some to another.

To judge a hypothesis, or to choose among two or more hypotheses, one needs standards or *criteria*. The first four criteria below are from the method used to judge scientific theories (Cohen & Nagel, 1934, pp. 207-215; Columbia Associates, 1923, pp. 59-61; Fearnside, 1980, pp. 242-245; Hall & Lindzey, 1957/1970, pp. 11-15; Lee, 1947).

1. **Comprehensiveness:**   It fits many of the facts of the case.

2. **Logical consistency:**   It makes sense.

3. **Predictive ability:**   It predicts new facts, or is consistent with new information that was not part of the original inference.

A choice between two competing theories or hypotheses can be made by setting up a *crucial experiment,* a situation in which one hypothesis predicts one outcome and the other predicts a different outcome. The 30-day trial in the resource room is a crucial experiment. Suppose the team cannot decide whether a student is learning disabled, or a late-blooming or disadvantaged child who will catch up without much trouble. On a trial period in the resource room, he catches on to decoding immediately. None of the usual students there learn so easily. The trial period has shown that he need not be identified as learning disabled, but needed only an extra boost to catch up with his class.

The criteria above apply to the reasoning or *means*. They can be judged by a set of rules that are the same for everyone. There are other criteria that involve to some degree the *values* or goals of reasoner and audience.

4. **Simplicity:**   If two theories are equally balanced in all other ways, preference goes to the simplest one (see Occam's Razor, Chapter 1, p. 6).

The principle of simplicity is an established scientific tradition that can be applied by anyone regardless of values. But the decision to use Occam's Razor implies an esthetic, or value judgment about the preferability of one explanation over another on grounds of taste — beauty (Columbia Associates, 1923, p. 53) or, in a word sometimes used by physical scientists, *elegance*. As with all values, it is hard to reason about taste. *De gustibus non est disputandum.*

5. **Value consistency:**   Science and technology are not value-free (Kuhn, 1962). They are inseparable from their wellsprings and their applications, and from questions about whether their achievements, including psychological testing, are good or bad for society.

There is an accepted value-system in educational and mental health organizations. As a practical matter, consultants must recognize this value-system for their work to be effective. "None of the Kallikaks can learn to read" is unacceptable; "cultural deprivation with hereditary learning disabilities" passes muster. The difference is more than verbal. The former allows no hope, whereas the latter only assigns low odds and modest goals.

The Test of Time

Time reveals the answer to many questions about children's development and potential, but we cannot usually afford to wait. One year will distinguish between the learning-disabled students and the late bloomers, but the second grade is too valuable a year to waste. If they need help and do not get it, there is more to lose than if they get help and do not need it.[10]

Time does, however, allow checking on past predictions and revising present ones accordingly. Even the much-maligned 3-year evaluations provide an opportunity for longitudinal observation of the progress of problem learners. "Remember Stevie? We thought he'd never learn to read, but he did. I saw him last week. He's 16 now. He's reading *Peyton Place*. It's not the world's greatest book, but he's reading it. If Stevie learned to read, this kid can too."

Part 2.
Application: Clinical Inference as It Is Done

CAN CLINICAL INFERENCE BE TAUGHT?

Long ago, Socrates was asked whether virtue can be taught.[11] One might as well ask whether any complex behavior that includes cognition, action, and value components can be taught. Clinical inference is such a behavior.

One of the problems in answering that question is the model of *teaching*. Today *teach* means *teach to anyone, regardless of capacity or motivation,* as in the third grade, or all the employees of the Widget Mfg. Co.

The original question predated universal compulsory education. In Socrates' day, education, other than military training, was more like today's graduate school. The students were a small, self-selected band of above-average people dedicated to learning. Teaching these students, unlike the broad, civic problem of public education, is the facilitation of learning in voluntary and active learners. To the extent that these conditions apply, we can teach virtue, or clinical inference, or perhaps anything else.

Speakers of colloquial English may be right, although incorrect, when they say "learn" for *teach*. "That'll *learn* you!" "Miss Baylson *learned* me English." A teacher is one who brings about learning.

The answer to the lead question is that clinical inference, and virtue, can be *learned*, although probably not by everyone. The teacher has the same relation to the skill learned as midwife to baby: a helping hand, but neither production nor full credit.

For Example: Jason Reconstituted and Others

Ten-year-old Jason was the hero of Chapter 2, which presents three levels of interpretation of his examination. The present chapter turns again to Jason's examination, this time as an example of the progress of clinical inference from rough examination notes to conclusions. His complete test report is reproduced for reference on pp. 133-136, at the end of the section on the logical process of integrating the data.

No one student, however, can serve as an example of all the points to be made about interpreting test data. Therefore selections from other students' examinations also appear, as needed.

ADDRESSING THE REFERRAL QUESTION

The referral question sets the *selective focus* that figures so prominently in some of the problem-solving models discussed above (*How the Internal Connection Is Discovered,* pp. 76-79).

The referral question determines what information will be collected: what observations will be done, who will be interviewed, what questions will be asked, what tests given, and the direction of the spotlight of the examiner's selective attention. In students' records, certain information will stand out, and in their test behavior, certain learning-related behaviors will stand out, because these data are either part of established syndromes or configurational webs, or they seem as though they might be part of others less familiar or established.

But the focus must not be too narrow. As discussed below (in *Beyond the Referral Question: The Practitioner's Responsibility,* pp. 145-147), the selective focus that serves the referral question should never become a set of blinders cutting off the clinician's view of the subject's development as a whole person.

The reason for Jason's referral was re-evaluation every 3 years to determine continued eligibility for special services as a learning-disabled student. Regarding 3-year updates as a routine chore overlooks several challenges in the situation: Children have not always previously been correctly diagnosed, especially if they were very young at the time. Organizational pressures act to maintain existing codes (see Chapter 3, p. 62), and testing may provide the only fresh appraisal available. Finally, testing offers longitudinal insight into the way learners who have encountered difficulties learn and fare (see *The Test of Time*, p. 82). Students already identified as handicapped are entitled to as much problem-solving attention on their behalf the second (or more) time around as the first.

Persons to interview would include Jason's classroom teacher and his resource room teacher. Tests would include a standard intelligence test and achievement tests in the basic tool skills. Reading the records, the examiner would pay particular attention to early childhood and medical information consistent with a constitutional or physical basis for learning difficulties; to the age when difficulties first surfaced, and the difficulties then described; to the hypotheses advanced by previous examinations to explain the difficulties. During the testing session, because Jason is coded learning disabled, the examiner would pay particular attention to behaviors often involved in learning disabilities: his language functioning — whether he receives communication efficiently and expresses ideas adequately; and his perceptual and motor behavior. During achievement testing, the examiner would pay particular attention to the smoothness of the decoding process; the use of context cues and the grasp of content in reading comprehension; the grasp of quantitative concepts, the automatic mastery of calculation, and the transformation of practical problems into calculation examples in math; in spelling, the relative use of phonics and visual memory in the encoding process; in written expression, the use of rules of writing mechanics, on one hand, and on the other, how long he takes to think of content, the level of language in which content is expressed, and the complexity of the thought content, especially in comparison with the understanding displayed on parts of the examination that do not require as much expressive facility.

Regardless of the referral question, the examiner should also consider Jason's development as a whole person; whether his life is working out well, and what part school plays in his success or failure in life.

THE MINOR PREMISES: GATHERING THE INFORMATION

The examiner begins by gathering a great deal of data, particular information. In the order encountered, they are background information, test behavior, and test scores. Many of these particulars will be linked to some general knowledge, like the minor premises of many syllogisms. The greater the amount of relevant information, the better the sample as a basis for conclusions.

Background Information

Background information — developmental and medical, family, interests and activities, school history, and previous tests — is often paid lip-service and treated as ritual required report-filler instead of essential information that can tighten the net of logical probability.

Developmental Information

Example 4-1 shows how Jason's developmental and medical history is weighed with respect to possible conclusions.

Example 4-1

Jason, 10-4, grade 4

Early Development and Medical:

Jason's mother was prescribed medication for difficulties during pregnancy. Jason was born in the posterior presentation. At 2 years, a fall caused a cut on the forehead, but he did not lose consciousness. At 2½ he had a high fever without convulsions. Developmental milestones were normal.

When Jason was 7-5, an optometrist found normal eyesight, but "multisensory difficulties that made school difficult."

When he was 8-1, a pediatric neurologist diagnosed developmental dyslexia.

Although Jason's early developmental information includes several risk factors, they do not add up to substantial evidence of central nervous system trauma. The information is inconclusive and should be kept in mind in relation to further information.

The medical information shows that at about the time of Jason's previous school examination, his parents also went to considerable effort and expense to take him to two outside experts. The optometrist's "multisensory difficulties" and the neurologist's "developmental dyslexia" may not be the examiner's categories, but they are strong statements and, especially together, represent a strong probability that there was "something wrong." The fact that his parents took him to them also tells something about their motivation and involvement as parents.

Example 4-2 shows how developmental and medical information combines with other kinds of information to tighten the net of logical probability in the inference of language learning disability. (This inference can be made by a learning examiner, and is not the same as a diagnosis of speech and language handicap, which requires a specialist in that area.)

[In examples to follow, rows of ellipsis points indicate material omitted as not relevant to the issue illustrated.]

Example 4-2

[12-1, grade 5]

. . . .

Early Development: She was born at 10 months of pregnancy, after prolonged induced labor, weighing 7 lb. Developmental milestones were normal. *She had chronic inner-ear problems with high temperatures. Age 4-7, tubes were inserted in her ears* and a tonsillectomy performed.

. . . .

School History:

She entered kindergarten at age 5-5. She spent a year in Readiness class. Her grades were fair: grade 1, mostly Bs, with C in spelling and E in language; grade 2, Bs and Cs. Yet November of grade 2, *she was referred for difficulty grasping concepts.* She had remedial reading in grades 3 and 4.

At the end of grade 3, she was coded learning disabled. She spent 7.5 hours a week in the resource room for written expression and math through grade 4. This year she spends 3.75 hours a week there, for written expression and academic support.

Previous Tests:

Age 6-0, on the school readiness test, she failed the hearing impedance test. She showed mixed dominance.

November of grade 2, age 8, on a reading screening test, her instructional reading level was 1^2 (primer).

Test Results:

Wechsler Intelligence Test for Children – Revised

(continued)

Example 4-2 *(continued)*

Verbal Scale IQ 86
Performance Scale IQ 95
Full Scale IQ 89

Significant strengths and weaknesses:
Similarities strong
Object Assembly weak

Memory for Sentences subtest from the Stanford-Binet IV 78

Achievements:

Reading:	GE	PR	SS
Decoding: WRAT-R, Level 1	3 End	7	78

Comprehension: Ekwall Reading Inventory
Silent Reading, Form D:
Grade 4 — Frustration Level
Difficulty understanding the oral questions affected this test
Oral Reading, Form C:
Grade 4 — Instructional Level
Grade 5 — Frustration Level
Reads aloud with excellent expression
Decoding unfamiliar words was a stumbling-block
Had difficulty understanding long sentences, if-clauses, and the relationship of dependent clauses to the main clause

Written Expression:

Spelling: Criterion-referenced, using the local curriculum standards: Grade 3

Writing Sample: Criterion-referenced, using local curriculum norms: Generally grade 5
Capitalization: Generally grade 5
Punctuation: Generally grade 5
Expression: Approaching grade 5
Could not think of a topic to write about
Given a topic, wrote fluently
Writes complete sentences (grade 2+)
Writes many run-on sentences (correcting these is a grade 4 to 6 skill)

Math: Criterion-referenced, using examples from the Brigance Inventory of Basic Skills and local curriculum standards: Grade 4

(continued)

Example 4-2 *(continued)*

Discussion:

. . . Although the WISC-R scores are not significant in this direction, the impression from the examination is a language learning disability. In addition to the vocabulary and comprehension difficulties on the Ekwall Reading Inventory described above, her verbal responses were either immediate or not-at-all, as though she had no internal monologue, but either makes an immediate association, or does not. Language problems are often found in people with early ear infections.

On the performance tasks, she did not use methodical approaches ("strategies"), but when frustrated, fell back on trial-and-error. This makes her a field-dependent learner, who needs learning structure and guides provided for her.

Summary: She appears to have difficulty understanding complex language, which often turns into difficulty with higher-order cognition, such as drawing inferences. Early developmental factors may have predisposed toward language difficulties. Her lack of internal monologue also affects her approach to hand–eye tasks, as she does not use problem-solving strategies, which internal monologue would support.

[Throughout the following text, excerpts from reports are italicized to indicate quotation from written sources.]

In Example 4-2, the pattern of achievement scores suggests language learning disability: Reading and some written expression skills are low while math approaches adequacy. The Verbal–Performance discrepancy cannot yet be interpreted as enough evidence of language learning disability as it is one point below the recommended level of significance.

Several pieces of nonquantitative information, however, add up to the needed logical evidence: Preschool history includes the *chronic ear infections* so often found with language problems. School history mentions *difficulty grasping concepts*. In this report format, the test results list related behaviors, which include *difficulty* in the following: *understanding oral questions, decoding unfamiliar words, understanding complex written langauge,* and *thinking of content for written expression.* More general learning-related behavior brought out in the discussion suggests *lack of internal monologue.* The ear infections are a possible cause of language problems, the behaviors possible signs.

This amount of nonquantitative evidence provides a convincing internal connection supporting the meaningfulness of a statistically nonsignificant score difference.

The examination eventually led to language therapy for her primary problem in addition to the academic help she had been receiving for her secondary one.

Living Situation

In Example 4-3, a sudden, dramatic academic improvement upon changing living situation appears at first to be an obvious result of that change.

Example 4-3

[14-9, grade 8]

Background Information: He gave the information that the occasion of his transfer to this district *a few weeks ago* was *his move from his father and step-mother's home to his mother and step-father's home. His mother left the family when he was 7 or 8.*

School History:

. . . He was referred and coded learning disabled in grade 5. He began this year at Suburban Heights High School with a program for 13 hours a week in the resource room. When he moved to this district, however, he was given a trial placement entirely in the mainstream, with resource room services available only on demand. He has done well academically without going to the resource room at all. He got B+ in English. He had some difficulty in Reading.

. . . .

Summary: He is a young man of normal intellectual ability. Although his test profile is consistent with the diagnosis he has borne in the past of a language learning disability, he no longer qualifies for this code because his achievements are grade level, even in those areas most vulnerable to learning disabilities.

The rapid adjustment from a relatively heavy special program to complete mainstream survival, and the lack of services in the early school history, suggested that living with his mother was the key to school achievement. When he lived with her, he did well at school, and when he lived with his father, he required special services.

Example 4-4

Jason, 10-4

Jason enjoys playing basketball, baseball, and soccer.

He likes to build things with batteries that make light bulbs light.

Example 4-5

Jason, 10-4, grade 4

In kindergarten, he "needed to work on motor skills." [This usually refers to crayons, pencil, and scissors.]

He was coded learning disabled at the end of grade 1, and has remained so ever since. Services have included speech/language.

In grade 2, his language-related tool skills were moved to the resource room. He now spends 7.5 hours a week there.

He does especially well on science projects, and just earned an A on one.

A brief passage of time again changed the picture. A few months later he moved back to his former home with his father. The staff never learned why he left a place where he appeared to be doing so well, whether he found the structure too unaccustomedly confining, or could not keep up with the mainstream demands, or some other reason they lacked the information to understand.

Interests and Activities

The out-of-school side of students often has implications for school learning.

← Jason's sports participation suggests good gross motor skills. It also suggests development of social group membership.

← Building things suggests good hand–eye skills for working with objects, although not necessarily pencils; in fact, sometimes there seems to be an inverse relationship. Batteries and light bulbs form a three-dimensional working system — a machine. These are the domain of people who are holistic rather than sequential. Jason's projects sound more complicated than most boys', and suggest above-average performance ability.

School History

Interpreting a school history requires some understanding of the way the particular school system deals with students. Jason's district tries hard to provide students with needed services.

← Needing to work on pencil and scissors skills in kindergarten is not necessarily predictive of a learning disability, but is consistent with one.

← Being coded in first grade is not reserved for the more serious problems in this district, where referrals are made early and the process runs smoothly.

← Better indications of seriousness are the increase in services the following year, and the present amount of time in the resource room. Speech/language services, and instruction in language-related tool skills (reading and written expression) in the resource room, suggest a language learning disability.

← Doing well on science projects is another sign of a holistic person. An A for a learning-disabled student shows unusual interest, ability, or both.

Example 4-6

[14-4, grade 7]

School History:

Before she entered school, her mother arranged an evaluation at the State Training School [for developmental disabilities] in their town [because most of the other children in the family are in special education]. Upon entering school, age 5-8, she received a code of mental retardation, and spent half a day in kindergarten and half at a day care center.

At the end of grade 1, she re-tested too high for her program. She repeated grade 1. In grade 2, she was coded learning disabled, and spent half days in a self-contained special class. In grade 3 she went to a learning disabilities resource room, and was discharged from that program. In grade 5, she was again referred for learning problems, and spent 4 hours a week in a learning disabilities resource room.

In junior high she has been in a self-contained special needs room. This year she is mainstreamed in math and science.

Previous Tests: Three IQ tests, ages 4 to 9, have shown scores ranging from 74 to 86.

Test Results:

Wechsler Intelligence Scale for Children — Revised
Verbal Scale IQ	86
Performance Scale IQ	101
Full Scale IQ	91

Wide-Range Achievement Test (administered by resource room teacher 2 weeks earlier)

Reading	4.7	Spelling	3.0	Math	4.3

. . . .

Summary: Her intellectual growth over the years should keep us from becoming discouraged with the fact that the categories of special education have not quite fitted her, so that she has had to be reclassified several times. Her program and her mother's supportiveness have helped her a great deal. She now clearly fits the pattern of a learning disabilities code. She has a foothold in the tool skills, but needs both remedial and supportive help.

Previous Tests

Previous tests, even more than developmental and family history, tend to be quoted, then ignored in drawing inferences. Yet by the time a student has had more than one test, the study has become longitudinal. To ignore the past is to give an incomplete picture of the present. Previous test results need to be integrated with present ones.

Example 4-6 has the happy task of explaining a rise in IQ.

← Many things cannot be said directly in a report. This family's difficulties included poverty, cultural deprivation, and familial mild mental retardation. Their assets included a competent mother who coped well with the situation.

← The student made enough progress in her first 2 years of school to be discharged from her code of mental retardation. Each time she was discharged, she soon needed services again, and was coded.

← The more restrictive program in junior high may have been imposed because it was feared that she could not cope with changing classes.

One factor in her many program changes might have been ability to master skills in due time, but great difficulty when new ones were introduced.

← Her present test scores show progress in overcoming the family IQ pattern. A rapid stage of adolescent development may have fueled the learning spurt. The Verbal–Performance discrepancy might be expected in view of the cultural deprivation.

← The many program changes, far from suggesting that she was programmed inappropriately, may show adaptations to her changing skills and developmental pace that have been instrumental to her progress.

A drop in IQ score, especially a large drop, needs to be explained. Example 4-7 shows Jason as typical of many learning-disabled students whose scores slip.

Example 4-7

Jason, 10-8, grade 4

Previous Tests:

Age 6-2, at his preschool screening, Jason failed the Preschool Speech and Language Test. The Gesell School Readiness Test found immature fine-motor skills.

Age 7-7, on a WISC-R, *Jason scored VSIQ 113, PSIQ 123, and FSIQ 120;* with significant strengths in Vocabulary and Mazes, and significant weaknesses in Digit Span and Picture Completion. A speech and language examination at that time showed age-appropriate vocabulary and concepts, but a 1-year lag in language processing and expressive language.

Test Results:

Wechsler Intelligence Scale for Children—Revised

    Verbal Scale IQ   95
    Performance Scale IQ   106
    Full Scale IQ   100

    Significant weakness: Coding

. . . .

Discussion: Jason's many learning disabilities, most of which do not show up in the test profile, and the quality of some of his responses, suggest that he is brighter than his present IQ scores show. The drop in scores since his last test often accompanies a learning disability, as the test content becomes increasingly school-influenced with age.

This example explains the drop in scores as being related to the detracting influence of his learning disabilities (see Chapter 3, p. 58), and the increasingly academic content of the test with age. It also mentions behavior that supports his higher previous score (*the quality of some of his responses*). Jason's parents might be expected to be achievement oriented on the basis of having taken him to outside specialists, and therefore to be upset by a drop in IQ score. If terms like "average" and "low average" are likely to upset parents, "normal" can be a better choice, implying merely the absence of retardation.

Other previous tests are also pertinent to the present examination. The Gesell *immature fine-motor skills,* which usually means pencil, may or may not be related to Jason's present difficulty in written expression. The Preschool Speech and Language Test, and the speech and language evaluation at age 7, suggest a language disability. The latter is quite specific, *processing and expressive language.* The intellectual component of language, *vocabulary* and *concepts,* has not been affected.

Collecting the Test Data

The selection of an appropriate test battery is beyond the scope of this discussion. Information about test selection is available from textbooks, supervisors, and colleagues.

Too Many Tests

The appropriate number of tests is more of a problem than it might appear. It may come as a surprise to those practitioners accustomed to overkill in testing that, in view of the statistical rule that increasing the number of samples also increases their likelihood of deviating from the mean, it is not only possible but easy to give too many tests, which result in *interpreting chance effects as real.* This is equivalent to performing too many statistical tests on the same research data, which increases the likelihood of finding statistical significance where none exists. (See Moore & McCabe, 1989, pp. 489-490.) Yet many teams wholeheartedly embrace the old medicine fallacy, "Little do good, more do better."

An examiner administers two different tests that sample the same general area, each with about 10 subtests — say the WISC-R and the Detroit Tests of Learning Aptitude — and uses the 95% level of confidence[12] to determine the significant strengths and weaknesses. *One* resulting subtest strength or weakness would be expected to be a fluke, a sampling error.

Suppose the examiner, after giving a subtest battery of customary length, say the whole WISC-R, wants to investigate further to check a hypothesis discovered during the examination — say, that the subject has difficulty catching and remembering spoken language. One way is to give some subtests in this area. If only one or two additional subtests are given, the likelihood of interpreting chance effects is not increased greatly.

Another way to investigate a suspected area of difficulty without increasing the risk of interpreting chance effects, is to *change the model of testing from statistical to clinical reasoning.* This can be done in two ways. One is to give additional tests that are criterion-referenced instead of norm-referenced, like those that compare language or pencil work samples with age standards. The other is to investigate the area pinpointed in behavior only. This might mean reviewing test behavior already observed to see if it holds an answer, eliciting new relevant behavior, or interviewing about areas of difficulty experienced.

There is something troubling about this issue: Accepted practice seems to break the too-many-tests rule continually. It is important to believe one's experience is valid. When textbooks conflict with experience, it is time to look carefully at both.

The evaluation of a new referral — say a first-grader — often involves three test batteries, if not four, by a learning specialist who may or may not be a school psychologist, a speech/language specialist, and an occupational therapist. The first provides a baseline of general ability, tests achievements to establish need, and may test learning modalities as well. The others test because their services may be needed, and require an examination by each. Sometimes there is a learning specialist in addition to a school psychologist, sometimes in cooperation but often in isolation from each other. Each of these three or four specialists gives at least 10 subtests, more often 20. By the time the testing is completed, from 30 to 80-plus subtests have been given.

All this might be statistically acceptable if each specialist tested a different pool of behaviors and did not exceed the limit for that pool. Achievement tests do not add to ability tests because they are intended to sample a different pool.

Lists of the tests actually given, however, raise some doubt about how separate the pools really are. The learning specialist overlaps with speech/language on vocabulary, comprehension, and auditory memory, and an occasional Illinois Test of Psycholinguistic Abilities, and overlaps with the occupational therapist on perceptual and motor skills. If there is a learning specialist in addition to a school psychologist, the overlap is almost complete. Of 80 overlapping subtests, perhaps 4 would be significant at the 95% level by chance alone, depending on the amount of overlap.

Sometimes additional tests are given in bad faith, from desire to prove learning disabilities against adequate contrary evidence. (See Chapter 6, p. 83.) Most of the time the team is simply trying to be as thorough and conscientious as possible.

Often one examiner gives too many tests. Sometimes the results are as haphazard as would be predicted. Yet some examiners regularly give too many, with sensible, consistent results. I was once asked to give a learning disabilities evaluation (not my specialty) to a child who had recently had the Stanford-Binet: Form L-M, which yields a unitary score relatively unaffected by many learning disabilities, and for the same reason is not geared to diagnosing them. The Binet L-M had by then been replaced by the 4th edition, but the examiner must have realized it was the only test on which this formerly abused and neglected foster child could score the 90 IQ needed for services. With a clear field, I composed a battery of favorite subtests from my own model of learning modalities, but neglected the too-many-tests rule and gave too many subtests! Yet they came out perfectly consistent with classroom and test behavior.

The answer may be that there is enough difference in total content between the whole pool sampled by tests of general ability that ask "Is *anything* the matter," and clearly delimited areas of the pool sampled by tests with causal hypotheses that ask "Is *this* the matter," that the too-many-tests rule does not apply to combining them. Otherwise, the problem of team testing vs. the too-many-tests rule may be one of those presently unexplained experiences, like unidentified rings in the grass and objects in the sky, that await new solutions.

Practitioners still need to be careful about administering too many subtests that cover the same territory, like the Wechsler and the Detroit Tests of Learning Aptitude. The additional information sought by overtesting can often be found in the learning-related test behavior.

Taking Behavioral Notes

The best place to start improving clinical inference is renewing attention to observing test behavior, and jotting down observations *at the time.*

Figure 4 reproduces the original notes taken during Jason's examination. They contain his answers to interview questions, other answers not recorded in test booklets, and test behavior. Some of the observations were circled at the time of writing to emphasize their diagnostic importance, originally in red pen to aid in scanning. Because of the semilegibility of the notes, the adjacent page gives the notes in print with personal shorthand spelled out. In the typeface version, notes about test behavior, both those originally circled and others, are italicized.

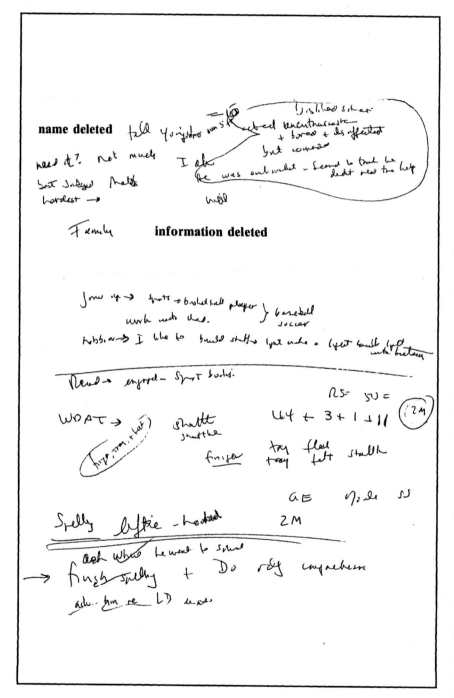

Figure 4. Original notes from Jason's examination.

Jason   *tall youngster over 5 ft   Disliked situation   acted*
   unenthusiastic   and bored and disaffected but cooperative

need it?   not much   I don't know   *He was ambivalent. Seemed*
   to think he didn't need the help

best subject   Math
hardest   [illegible even to the writer]

Family   [information deleted]

grow up   sports   basketball player   baseball   soccer
[what if you couldn't do that?]   work with dad

hobbies   I like to build stuff   light   make a light bulb light with
   battery

Read   enjoyed   Sport books

WRAT[-R]   44 + 3 + 1 + [2]   RS = 50 = 2M

   shultt   [probably refers to attempts
   shuttle   to pronounce *should*]

		try	flet	
finger, tray, + felt	*finiger*	tray	felt	stallk
	GE	%ile	SS	
	2M			

Spelling   *leftie — hooked*

[in the writer's shorthand, this means end of first session; below list
of things to do next session]

Ask where he went to school

finish spelling + Do reading comprehension

ask him re LD [illegible]

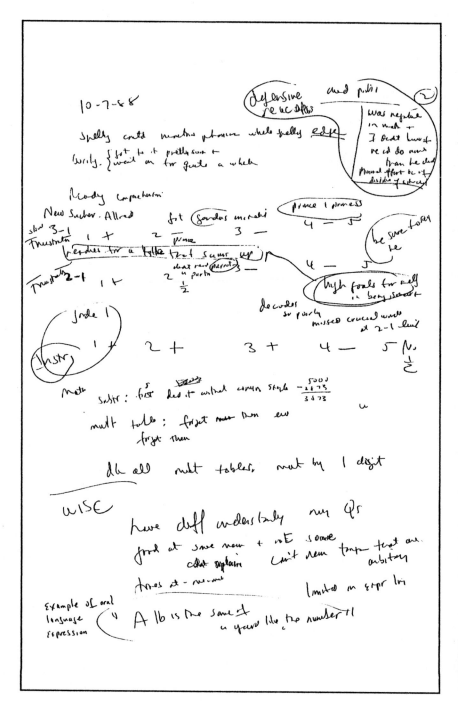

Figure 4 (continued).

10-7-88 [second session]

defensive re ac[ademic] diff[icultie]s
aud[itory] prob[lem]s
was negative in math + I didn't know if he c[oul]d do more than he did
Minimal effort because of dislike of situation

Spelling cont[inue]d   *mouths phonics while spelling* **edge**

Writing   *got to it pretty soon + went on for quite a while*

Reading comprehension

New Sucher-Allred [Reading Placement Inventory]

slow 3-1   *got genders mixed   prince + princess*
Frustration [level]
    1 +   2 −   3 −   4 −   5   be sure to say he [?]
              prince
     reaches for a title that sums up   high goals for self in being smart

2-1   1 +   2 ½ *a parta*   3 −   4 −   5 −
              didn't read ***parrot***
Frustration [level]
        decodes so poorly missed crucial words at 2-1 level

Grade 1
    1 +   2 +   3 +   4 −   5 ½
Instr[uctional level]   No

Math   5000
    subtr[action]: first did it without copying example   − 2873
       [page of example shows correct answer]   3873
    Mult[iplication] table: forget them   [illegible]
                  forget them
    d[oesn't] k[now] all mult[iplication] tables. mu[l]t[iplies] by 1 digit

---

WISC [-R]

have difficulty understanding my Qs
good at some mem[ory] + not some   c[ou]ldn[']t explain   can't
   rem[ember] things that are arbitrary
tries at one-word [this probably refers to trying to answer the
   Similarities subtest items with one-word responses]
limited in expr[essive] lang[uage]
"A lb is the same of a yard like the number."

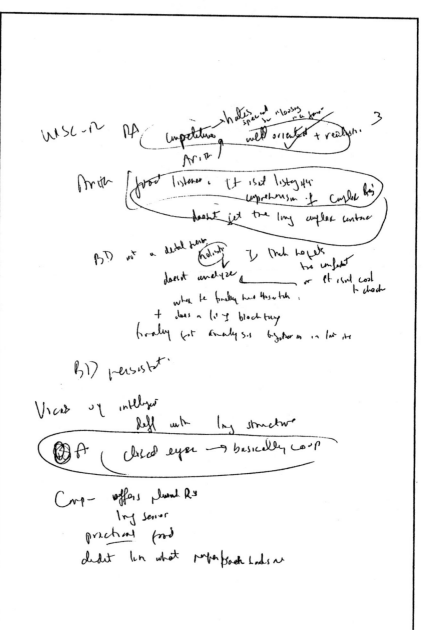

Figure 4 (continued).

WISC-R

P[icture] A[rrangement]   *competitive   well oriented + realistic*

[an arrow from *competitive* to] *hates spec[ial] ed[ucation] bc*
[because] "losing in a game"

Arith[metic] [an arrow from "Arith" to "competitive" indicates
that Jason also acted competitive on the Arithmetic subtest]

Arith[metic]   *good listener. It isn't listening it's comprehension*
of complex lang[uage]   doesn't get the long complex sentences

B[lock] D[esign]   *not a detail person   holistic   doesn't analyze*
I think he gets too confident or it isn't cool to check
when he finally had to switch [from holistic to analytic method]
+ does a lot of block turning
finally got analysis together in last item
BD persistent

Vocab[ulary]   *v[er]y intelligent   diff[iculty] with language structure*

O[bject] A[ssembly]   *closed eyes* [while the pieces were being put out
behind the screen] [arrow indicates "therefore"] *basically cooperative*

Comp[rehension]   *offers plural Rs* [this indicates without being
queried]
long series [of responses offered in response to the same item]
practical good [indicates he did especially well on the more
practical items]
didn't kn[ow] what paperback books are

Here is the behavioral data extracted from the examination notes.

Interview

Tall youngster, over 5 ft.

Disliked situation. Acted unenthusiastic and bored and disaffected, but cooperative.

He was ambivalent [about needing resource room]. Seemed to think he didn't need the help, then said he didn't know.

He thinks his best subject is math.

When he grows up, he would like to do the same work as his dad [technical specialty].

Hobby: likes to build things with batteries that make light bulbs light.

Achievements

Reading decoding errors show difficulty with one-syllable words with blends.

In reading comprehension, he decoded so poorly that he could not understand the 2-1 passage; but tried hard to find a title that summarizes the passage. This shows he has high goals for himself in being smart.

He is left-handed with a hooked pencil hold.

While spelling a difficult one-syllable word with two medial consonants, he subvocalized.

Given an open-ended writing assignment, he applied himself without hesitation [although he did not produce much].

In math, he tried to do a difficult subtraction example without writing it down, and got it wrong. When he copied it, he got it right.

WISC-R

On the WISC-R, he had difficulty understanding my questions.

He was good at some memory tasks and not good at some, and couldn't explain the difference. I thought he couldn't remember things that are arbitrary.

He tried to give one-word answers on the Similarities subtest.

He appears limited in expressive language.

As an example of his language expression, he said, "A pound is the same of a yard like the number."

On Picture Arrangement, he was competitive, well-oriented, and realistic.

He was also competitive on Arithmetic.

Hates special education because it is "losing in a game."

On Arithmetic, he was a good listener.

His difficulty isn't listening in itself; it's comprehension of complex language. He doesn't get the long complex sentences.

On Block Design, he is not a detail person. He is holistic. He doesn't analyze. I think he gets too confident, or it isn't "cool" to check his work. When he finally had to switch from the holistic to analytic

method, because the items got too difficult to see the answer right
away, he did a lot of block-turning (trial and error), and finally used
an analytic approach on the last item.
He was persistent on Block Design.
On Vocabulary, he gave the impression of being very intelligent, but
had difficulty with language structure. (This refers to responses that
are not grammatical, or grammatically parallel to the stimulus word.)
On Object Assembly, he closed his eyes while the pieces were being put
out behind the screen, showing his basic cooperativeness.
On Comprehension, he offered spontaneous plural responses, sometimes
several of them. He did especially well on the more practical items.

The Pitfall of Behavioral Description: The Behavioral Concrete Report

Some examiners do an excellent job observing and describing
behavior — and stop there. Their reports read like the above list written in paragraph form. The conclusions might resemble the Level 2
report — ability classification; significant discrepancy, strengths, and
weaknesses; and underachievement or not. But the behavior has not
entered into the conclusions.

This is another kind of concrete report: the behavioral concrete
report. Behavioral information is given but not interpreted.

Sometimes the behavioral concrete report shows a thorough and
observant examiner who lacks general knowledge or the integrative
ability or self-confidence to draw conclusions. Occasional islands of
uninterpreted behavior can mean, even emphasize, that the examiner
has drawn a blank. This is perfectly acceptable. No one knows everything.

Behavioral concreteness can also be an avoidance ploy, a sign that
the examiner does not wish to become involved in the issues at hand.
Here is an occasion when I needed this ploy:

[17-1] This young man's hair was cut in a Mohawk, with a tail in addition.
He did not look as if he was in good physical condition. He explained
his appearance by saying he had only had a few hours of sleep the night
before. However, when I spoke to his mother on the phone, she said
that on the contrary, he had gone to bed early and slept very soundly
all night.

I suspected the young man's condition was a result of taking drugs.
If I had said this in the report, the school authorities would have felt
obligated to take administrative action, and I would have been legally
liable. Everyone involved with him had already reached the same

conclusion. Therefore I merely recorded the observation of some apparent but unexplained physical factor interfering with his application.

THE MAJOR PREMISES: THE ROLE OF KNOWLEDGE

The Necessity of Knowledge

The data of the examination can only lead to conclusions when the examiner has the background of knowledge to give them meaning. That is why the examiner needs to be an educated person. Each minor premise must be connected with a major premise, the general knowledge that includes the case and helps explain it. This book cannot provide the major premises, the knowledge needed. That knowledge is in books about child development, learning, and pathology. It is not limited to facts. Theories are also essential equipment. Knowledge comes not only from books, courses, and conferences, but also informally, from colleagues and from the children, by continually building on knowledge by the interaction of knowledge with daily experience.

Knowledge should not be primarily about tests. Knowledge limited to tests produces test-centered, or test-population-centered conclusions. In society's haste to provide the many examiners needed, people have been trained to give tests without being educated about what they are testing for. Knowledge about learning and pathology provides insight into the inner connection between test scores and test behavior. Developmental and sociological knowledge illuminates background information, school history, and previous tests.[13]

New and Unpublished Knowledge

Many practitioners have a fund of unpublished knowledge, that may have been passed along by teachers and colleagues, or may be the practitioner's own discovery. "When kids do this, it's usually a sign of. . . ." "The people in this area tend to be. . . ." Informal knowledge is not unprofessional. As the change in Kaufman's Practitioners' Rules (Chapter 1, p. 9) illustrates, knowledge is never complete or finished. New knowledge can come from any source. One need not have status to make a contribution.

Some psychologists are scornful of informal knowledge. However, all organizational cultures use some informal knowledge, and on occasion accept even more, from regard for its logical force or respect for the speaker. The standards for informal knowledge are no more nonexistent or vague than any other group of social standards.

It is particularly important to make use of unique knowledge of local culture. The children have a right to have someone understand and consider their way of life.

Two Examples

As an example of informal, unpublished knowledge, Figures 5 and 6 show two Wechsler Block Design signs, discovered but never verified by investigation. Some subjects do something similar to Figure 5. This response first came to my attention in an acting-out child. Symbolism is the hypothesis that small, insignificant acts are similar to larger, more significant ones. This construction of the design, out of the bounds of the pattern outline, mirrored his out-of-bounds behavior. Most of the subsequent children who made this response were also acting-out children, leading to the name, the Out-of-Bounds Solution.

Figure 6 was dubbed the Creative Alternative. It isn't right, but it isn't completely wrong either. The subject has grasped the elements of the design, but has not followed the relationship of the design to the field: the design is lifted out of its context, the field rotated. The

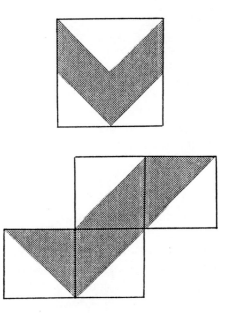

Figure 5. "There aren't anough blocks!" The Out-of-Bounds Solution. Wechsler Intelligence Scale for Children—Revised. Copyright © 1974 by The Psychological Corporation. Reproduced by permission. All rights reserved.

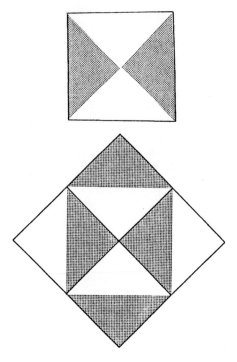

Figure 6. The Creative Alternative. Wechsler Intelligence Scale for Children — Revised. Copyright © 1974 by The Psychological Corporation. Reproduced by permission. All rights reserved.

performance is reminiscent of the changes in size, position, and part-whole relationship seen in certain pencil errors. Yet the solution looks more difficult than the original problem. Because of its originality, complexity, and independence from context, it seems creative and holistic.

New Categories

The most important kind of new knowledge is the conceptualization of new categories. As society changes, people behave differently. When services address groups never before served, current ways of thinking do not help understand or remedy their problems. *Attention deficit* and *cultural influences* were conceptualized to meet such needs.

Practitioners need to keep eyes and minds open for new categories to describe occurrences that present categories do not account for. Categories do not have to be exhaustive — apply to everyone, or exclusive — no overlap, as long as they are useful. When presented with a set of canned categories made up by someone else, the practitioner should always question whether they represent the best way of looking at the data, or whether they can be improved, or should be replaced.

Unplanned Obsolescence: When Knowledge Grows Old

Conclusions can later be rendered incorrect by scientific progress that disproves the underlying general knowledge. The example that recurs in this book is the change in Kaufman's Practitioners' Rules, which changed the interpretation of Jason's Coding score from *significantly weak* to *not significantly weak.* In individualized interpretation, this particular change makes very little difference in the total picture, because the scores are cross-checked against all the other information, as on pp. 80-82. More resounding changes are that psychologists no longer believe that every 20-point Verbal–Performance discrepancy indicates brain damage, or that a 75 IQ score alone denotes mental retardation. These false premises make conclusions from them wrong if there is not additional evidence. The term [mild] *brain damage* was once equivalent to the present *learning disabilities,* but resulted in little treatment, although people who found out their own diagnosis might suffer self-concept damage. Past misdiagnoses of retardation, however, could be self-fulfilling by resulting in treatment that reinforced them.

There is a rule in logic that reasoning from false premises yields conclusions that, although wrong, are still *valid,* that is, they follow logically from their premises. We are all limited by the state of scientific knowledge of our time, as well as by our own knowledge.

GETTING IT TOGETHER: INTEGRATING THE DATA IN SEARCH OF INTERNAL CONNECTION

The inference process has two sides: a logical side that moves in a straight and public course from data to conclusions, and a psychological side with a more individual and winding path.

The Logical Process

The Data Reviewed

The starting point of the process is the information from Jason's examination. It is reviewed below in the order in which the examiner discovers it: background information, test behavior, and test results.

Background Information

Early Development and Medical

Mother was prescribed medication for difficulties during pregnancy. Birth in posterior presentation.

At 2 yrs, fall caused cut on forehead, but he did not lose consciousness.

At 2½ he had a high fever without convulsions.

Developmental milestones normal.

Age 7-5, optometrist found normal eyesight but "multisensory difficulties that made school difficult."

Age 8-1, pediatric neurologist diagnosed "developmental dyslexia."

Family

Sister, 12. Both parents in the home, both employed.

Activities, Interests

Plays basketball, baseball, soccer.

Likes to build things with batteries that make light bulbs light.

School History

Kindergarten, "needed to work on motor skills." [usually pencil, etc.]

Coded LD end of grade 1 until present.

Has had speech/language.

In grade 2, language-related tool skills moved to resource room.

Spends 7.5 hrs/wk in resource room.

Does especially well on science projects, just got A on one.

Previous Tests

Age 6-2, preschool screening, failed Preschool Speech/Language Test. Gesell found immature fine-motor skills.

Age 7-7, WISC-R, VSIQ 113, PSIQ 123, FSIQ 120. Strengths, Vocabulary, Mazes; weaknesses, Digit Span, Picture Completion.

Age 7-7, speech/language exam, age-appropriate vocabulary and concepts, 1-yr lag in language processing and expressive language.

Behavioral Notes

Interview

Tall youngster, over 5 ft.

Disliked situation. Acted unenthusiastic and bored and disaffected, but cooperative.

He was ambivalent [about needing resource room]. Seemed to think he didn't need the help, then said he didn't know.

He thinks his best subject is math.

When he grows up, he would like to do the same work as his dad [technical specialty].

Hobby: likes to build things with batteries that make light bulbs light.

Achievements

Reading decoding errors show difficulty with one-syllable words with blends.

In reading comprehension, he decoded so poorly that he could not understand the 2-1 passage; but tried hard to find a title that summarizes the passage. This shows he has high goals for himself in being smart.

He is left-handed with a hooked pencil hold.

While spelling a difficult one-syllable word, he subvocalized.

Given an open-ended writing assignment, he applied himself without hesitation [although he did not produce much].

In math, he tried to do a difficult subtraction example without writing it down, and got it wrong. When he copied it, he got it right.

WISC-R

On the WISC-R, he had difficulty understanding my questions.

He was good at some memory tasks and not good at some, and couldn't explain the difference. I thought he couldn't remember things that are arbitrary.

He tried to give one-word answers on the Similarities subtest.

He appears limited in expressive language.

As an example of his language expression, he said, "A pound is the same of a yard like the number."

On Picture Arrangement, he was competitive, well-oriented, and realistic.

He was also competitive on Arithmetic.

Hates special education because it is "losing in a game."

On Arithmetic, he was a good listener.

His difficulty isn't listening in itself; it's comprehension of complex language. He doesn't get the long complex sentences.

On Block Design, he is not a detail person. He is holistic. He doesn't analyze. I think he gets too confident, or it isn't "cool" to check his work. When he finally had to switch from the holistic to analytic method, because the items got too difficult to see the answer right away, he did a lot of block-turning (trial and error), and finally used an analytic approach on the last item.

He was persistent on Block Design.

On Vocabulary, he gave the impression of being very intelligent, but had difficulty with language structure. (This refers to responses that are not grammatical, or grammatically parallel to the stimulus word.)

On Object Assembly, he closed his eyes while the pieces were being put out behind the screen, showing his basic cooperativeness.

On Comprehension, he offered spontaneous plural responses, sometimes several of them. He did especially well on the more practical items.

Test Results

Wechsler Intelligence Scale for Children — Revised
(IQ scores 90-109 and scaled scores 8-11 are in the average range. W
shows a subtest significantly weak for its subscale.)

Verbal Tests		Performance Tests	
Information	10	Picture Completion	12
Similarities	8	Picture Arrangement	11
Arithmetic	9	Block Design	11
Vocabulary	9	Object Assembly	13
Comprehension	10	Coding	8 W
(Digit Span)	(7)		

Verbal Scale IQ	95	Performance Scale IQ	106
	Full Scale IQ	100	

Achievements:

Reading:	Grade Equivalent	Percentile Rank	Standard Score
Decoding: WRAT-R, Level 1	2 Mid.	1	65

Comprehension: New Sucher-Allred Reading Placement Inventory
  Instructional Level: Grade 1
  Frustration Level: Grade 2
  See comments under Discussion below

Written Expression:

Spelling: WRAT-R, Level 1	2 Beg.	2	69

Writing sample, criterion-referenced, using standards from the
    local curriculum
  Capitalization: Inconsistent mastery of first word
    (grade 1)
  Expression: Beginning grade 3
    Writes and recognizes complete sentence (grade 2+)
    Writes short story in proper sequence (grade 2+)
  Language: Below thought level shown elsewhere (grade 2 to 3)
  Handwriting: Uses cursive script (grade 4)

Math: Criterion-referenced, using examples from the Brigance
  Inventory of Basic Skills, and standards from local curriculum:
  Grade 4, gap at grade 3
    Multidigit subtraction with borrowing (grade 3+)
    Multiplication facts need refreshing (grade 3)
    Multiplies 3 digits × 1 digit with carrying (grade 4)

The Chain of Reasoning

The order in which information is discovered is also the order in which the examiner begins to draw inferences.

Background Information

Several kinds of background information about Jason appear throughout pp. 85-95 with interpretive commentary. Table 6 summarizes this information and shows its logical structure by presenting it in brief reversed-premises syllogism form. (See pp. 67-68.) The columns show the particular information, the general knowledge applicable to each particular, and the conclusion. The rows follow each piece of information to conclusion. Some of the conclusions are reached by combining several pieces of particular information, a process of induction (see pp. 72-75).

Informal Judgments of Probability

Clinical reasoning includes an informal quantification, expressed in such phrases as *occasionally, sometimes, often, usually* or *probably, very often* or *quite likely,* and *almost always* or *very highly likely,* as seen in Table 6. The relative weight given various pieces of information changes in response to professional experience and scientific discovery; it has been my experience that these informal probabilities change even more readily than other kinds of general knowledge.

Some conclusions are reached by combining several pieces of information, a process of induction (see pp. 72-75) that includes informal quantitative judgments such as how many *oftens* make a *very highly likely* in the case under consideration.

Behavioral Notes: Level of Abstraction

Clinicians should be aware of the level of abstraction they use in their notes, although there is no need to hew to the lowest level of *Psych 101.* (See Chapter 2, p. 22.)

My own categories of level of abstraction are: *objective observations, inferred states of mind, generalized descriptions,* and *explanations.* The notes on Jason are categorized below:

(1) **Objective Observations.** These include Jason's statements, occasionally rephrased by the examiner.

Tall youngster, over 5 ft.
Seemed to think he didn't need the help, then said he didn't know.
He thinks his best subject is math.

Table 6
Reasoning from Background Information to Conclusions

Particular information	General knowledge	Conclusions
Mother was prescribed medication for difficulties during pregnancy.	This is an inconclusive risk factor.	None
Jason was born in the posterior presentation.	This is an inconclusive risk factor.	None
Age 2 years, a fall caused a cut on the forehead, but he did not lose consciousness.	This is an inconclusive risk factor.	None
Age 2½ years, he had a high fever without convulsions.	This is an inconclusive risk factor.	None
Developmental milestones were normal.	People with normal developmental milestones usually test above the range of mental retardation.	Ability is probably above range of mental retardation.
Age 7-5, an optometrist found normal eyesight, but "multisensory difficulties that made school difficult."	Children with these optometric findings are often learning disabled.	This is somewhat suggestive of learning disabilities.
	Parents who take their children to perception-oriented optometrists are often achieving and involved.	Maybe I had better watch my step on this one.
Age 8-1, a pediatric neurologist diagnosed developmental dyslexia.	Children with this diagnosis are quite likely to be learning disabled.	This is quite suggestive of learning disabilities.

(continued)

Table 6 *(Continued)*

Particular information	General knowledge	Conclusions
	Parents who take their children to pediatric neurologists are highly likely to be achieving and involved.	On top of the optometrist, yet! I had *really* better watch my step.
He enjoys playing basketball, baseball, and soccer.	Children who play these sports usually have good gross-motor coordination.	Jason probably has good gross-motor coordination.
	Competitive sports provide a good opportunity for social group membership.	He is probably developing social group membership.
He likes to build things with batteries that make light bulbs light.	People who like to build things usually have good hand–eye skills (but not necessarily for pencils).	He probably has good hand–eye skills (but not necessarily for pencils).
	People who build machines are almost always holistic rather than sequential.	He is highly likely to be holistic rather than sequential.
In kindergarten, he "needed to work on motor skills." [This usually refers to crayon, pencil, and scissors.]	Some kindergartners who "need to work on motor skills" are learning disabled and some are not.	Although consistent with a learning disability, this is inconclusive in itself.
He was coded learning disabled at the end of grade 1 . . .	Students who were coded usually qualified for their code.	He probably was learning disabled in grade 1.
. . . and has remained so ever since.	Organizational forces tend to maintain existing codes.	I need to keep an open mind to the possibility that the picture has changed, or that he was misdiagnosed.

(continued)

Table 6 (Continued)

Particular information	General knowledge	Conclusions
Services have included speech/language.	Learning-disabled students who have had speech/language services are sometimes language learning disabled.	He might be language learning disabled.
In grade 2, his language-related tool skills were moved to the resource room.	Students whose resource room time is increased have more serious needs than staff originally thought.	He turned out to have more serious problems than staff originally thought.
	Students who have language-related tool skills in the resource room are likely to be language learning disabled.	This strengthens the probability concluded above, from speech/language services, of a language learning disability.
He now spends 7.5 hours per week there.	The standard kid coded LD spends 3.75 hours per week. More time means a more serious problem.	This really doesn't add to the probability of seriousness already suggested by moving language-related tool skills there, because it is another way of saying the same thing.
He does especially well on science projects and just earned an A on one.	People who are good at science *and* at projects are quite likely to be holistic.	This goes with building machines toward strongly suggesting that he is holistic. The machine described above might have been the science project too, but either way, this is strong evidence.

(continued)

Table 6 *(Continued)*

Particular information	General knowledge	Conclusions
He failed the preschool speech and language test.	A lot of kids fail those tests.	This is consistent with the language indications above, but not particularly conclusive.
The Gesell found immature fine-motor skills.	Some kids with this finding are learning disabled and some are immature.	None
Age 7-7, WISC-R scores were VSIQ 113, PSIQ 123, FSIQ 120.	I have found Wechsler scores below age 8 somewhat unstable.	He is probably pretty bright, but take those scores with a grain of salt.
Significant strengths, Vocabulary and Mazes; weaknesses, Digit Span and Picture Completion.	Generic meanings are: Vocabulary with those weak language signs probably means good thinking; Mazes good planning; Digit Span weak auditory recall for meaningless material; Picture Completion weak detail work. Vocabulary is the most stable subtest.	Try those on for size, especially good thinking.
Speech/language exam: age-level vocabulary and concepts, but 1-year lag in processing and expression.	In certain people, receptive and expressive difficulties do not affect thought.	From this and other language findings and IQ scores, he sounds like a language learning–disabled good thinker.

When he grows up, he would like to do the same work as his dad [technical specialty].

Hobby: Likes to build things with batteries that make light bulbs light.

Reading decoding errors show difficulty with one-syllable words with blends.

In reading comprehension, he decoded so poorly that he could not understand the 2-1 passage.

He is left-handed with a hooked pencil hold.

While spelling a difficult one-syllable word, he subvocalized.

Given an open-ended writing assignment, he applied himself without hesitation [although he did not produce much].

In math, he tried to do a difficult subtraction example without writing it down and got it wrong. When he copied it, he got it right.

He was good at some memory tasks and not good at some, and couldn't explain the difference.

He tried to give one-word answers on the Similarities subtest.

As an example of his language expression, he said, "A pound is the same of a yard like the number."

He did a lot of block-turning.

He was persistent on Block Design.

On Vocabulary . . . he had difficulty with language structure.

On Object Assembly, he closed his eyes while the pieces were being put out behind the screen.

On Comprehension, he offered spontaneous plural responses, sometimes several of them.

(2) Inferred States of Mind. Inferred states of mind are more subjective than objective observations, but it is quite possible to get agreement on them. In psychology this agreement is called *interrater reliability*. In philosophy it is called *intersubjective testability* or *public behavior* (Feigl, 1958, pp. 387-409).

Disliked situation. Acted unenthusiastic and bored and disaffected but cooperative.

He was ambivalent [about needing resource room].

. . . tries hard to find a title that summarizes the passage.

On the WISC-R, he had difficulty understanding my question.

On Picture Arrangement, he was competitive, well-oriented, and realistic.

He was also competitive on Arithmetic.

On Arithmetic, he was a good listener.

On Block Design, he is not a detail person. . . . When he finally had to switch from the holistic to the analytic method, because the items got too difficult to see the answer right away, he did a lot of [block-turning] trial and error, and finally used an analytic approach on the last item.

Objective observations and inferred states of mind are both treated the same way, as the data of observation. The difference between them is that it is easier to be wrong about another's state of mind.

(3) **Generalized Descriptions.** These generalizations about an individual's behavior or state of mind, based on small samples of behavior, are discussed on p. 74.

> This shows he has high goals for himself in being smart.
> I thought he couldn't remember things that are arbitrary.
> He appears limited in expressive language.
> He is holistic. He doesn't analyze [until forced to].
> On Vocabulary he gave the impression of being very intelligent.
> [On Object Assembly, he closed his eyes while the pieces were being put out behind the screen,] showing his basic cooperativeness.
> On Comprehension . . . he did especially well on the more practical items.

Some generalizations about an individual's behavior are relatively simple and of obvious derivation (*he appears limited in expressive language*). [Excerpts from notes are italicized like those from reports.] Others are more complex and difficult to reconstruct (*he is holistic*). There follows an explanation of the derivation of this complex behavioral generalization.

On the Wechsler Block Design subtest, there are subjects who, upon first being presented with the blocks and the stimulus card, immediately push all four blocks together at once to make the design, without appearing to look at the card long enough to analyze the design, or to pay any attention to the separate blocks at all. There! This is the person who does things by wholes instead of in parts. When the design becomes more complicated and cannot be grasped intuitively, errors begin to occur. One place is WISC-R item 7, the first item with asymmetrical diagonals. Another is the first 9-block design, another the second 9-block design where the design has no lines in common with the block boundaries.

There are many other behaviors that can reflect a holistic approach, like global reading decoding errors and difficulty spelling, but on Block Design it is visible in action.

(4) **Explanations.**

> Hates special education because it is "losing in a game."
> His difficulty isn't listening in itself; it's comprehension of complex language. He doesn't get the long complex sentences.
> I think he gets too confident, or it isn't "cool" to check his work.

When the level of abstraction of a behavioral note is *generalized description* or *explanation,* the inference process has begun before the note was written. This often happens when an experienced examiner swings into action at the test scene. Some conclusions are reached immediately without thinking. The whole examination, however, eventually requires conscious inference.

Behavioral Notes: The Links in the Chain

The particular information in behavioral notes includes objective observations and inferred states of mind. Generalized descriptions serve as both inductive conclusions and particular information. They are the small-sample inductive conclusions discussed on p. 74 (*he had difficulty with one-syllable words and blends* on this passage, therefore *he has difficulty decoding* in general). Generalized descriptions can also serve as stepping-stones to further conclusions by linking up with general knowledge (*students who have difficulty decoding are often learning disabled,* therefore *he may well be learning disabled*).

Table 7
Reasoning from Observations to Conclusions

Particular information	
Objective observations	Inferred states of mind
Tall youngster, over 5 ft.	
	Disliked situation. Acted unenthusiastic and bored and disaffected . . .
	. . . but cooperative.
Seemed to think he didn't need the help [this is probably based on response to interview question], *then said he didn't know.*	*He was ambivalent* [about needing resource room].

Table 7 shows the reasoning links between each observation, state of mind, and generalized description found in the behavioral notes on Jason (pp. 113, 118-119), the general knowledge applicable to each particular, and the resulting conclusion. Some conclusions are explanations, and some are higher-order generalizations — statements that integrate several pieces of information (*he has difficulty expressing himself on the level of his understanding*). The columns show the particular information, the general knowledge, and the conclusions. The rows follow each piece of information to its conclusion.

Some of the conclusions in Table 7 combine several pieces of information by inductive reasoning. This information comes not only from the behavioral notes but also from the background information already known. Some of the conclusions in Table 7 are therefore derived in part from information in Table 6 (pp. 114-117), because each step of inference builds on all preceding knowledge.

Small-sample inductive conclusions that can also serve as particular information	General knowledge	Conclusions
Generalized descriptions	General knowledge	Explanations and higher-order generalizations
Must be in early preadolescence. HE FELT NEGATIVE ABOUT BEING TESTED. Disliked anything associated with special services.	Preadolescents dislike obvious dependence on adults.	Preadolescence may be a factor in dislike of special services.
 HE DISLIKES NEEDING SPECIAL SERVICES.	Expression and control of feelings are learned in the home.	Brought up to show his feelings, but "behave."

(continued)

Table 7 *(Continued)*

Particular information	
Objective observations	Inferred states of mind

He thinks his best subject is math.

When he grows up he would like to . . . [work in a technical specialty]. Hobby: Builds things with batteries that make light bulbs light.

Reading decoding errors show difficulty with one-syllable words with blends.

In reading comprehension, he decoded so poorly that he could not understand the 2-1 passage; . . .

| | *. . . [despite reading difficulty] he tried hard to find a title that summarizes the passage.* |

He is left-handed with a hooked pencil hold.

While spelling a difficult one-syllable word, he subvocalized.

| *Given an open-ended writing assignment, he applied himself without hesitation and persevered.* | Repeats the cooperation theme. |

[did not produce much]

Small-sample inductive conclusions that can also serve as particular information	General knowledge	Conclusions
Generalized descriptions	General knowledge	Explanations and higher-order generalizations
	Students best at math are sometimes LD.	Consistent with LD but not conclusive.
	Engineer-type males are often LD.	Consistent with LD but not conclusive. The odds are building.
DECODING IS A SERIOUS PROBLEM FOR JASON. He is having greater difficulty in reading than expected in his grade.	Students who have difficulty decoding are often LD.	Adds greatly to the LD odds.
READING COM-PREHENSION IS SEVERELY LIMITED BY DECODING.	Students who have difficulty decoding and comprehending reading material are often LD.	This is a result of the above rather than a separate finding.
This shows he has high goals for himself in being smart.	Small behaviors reflect larger, more important behavior.	
	Left handers with hooked hold are holistic and seem disproportionately LD.	More evidence he is holistic. Consistent with LD but not conclusive.
Sequential activities are difficult for him.	Spelling is a sequential task.	HIS HOLISTIC STYLE IS NOT COMPATIBLE WITH BEING A GOOD SPELLER.
Good motivation and effort on an autonomous task.		[The report does not mention that he is trying hard on a task difficult for him.]
Low productivity in written language.	Low productivity in written language can be caused by pencil difficulties or language difficulties.	Not ready to decide which of the two.

(continued)

Table 7 *(Continued)*

Particular information

Objective observations	Inferred states of mind
In math, he tried to do a difficult subtraction example without writing it down and got it wrong. When he copied it, he got it right.	This appears to be the result of overconfidence and competitiveness.
	On the WISC-R, he had difficulty understanding my questions [apparently refers to subtests before Arithmetic: Information and Similarities].
He was good at some memory tasks and not good at some, and couldn't explain the difference [missed Information items on states and numbers].	
He tried to give one-word answers on the Similarities subtest.	
[His language responses were brief and grammatically simple.]	
As an example of his language expression, he said, "A pound is the same of a yard like the number."	

Small-sample inductive conclusions that can also serve as particular information	General knowledge	Conclusions
Generalized descriptions	General knowledge	Explanations and higher-order generalizations
		He knows he is bright at some things, and tries to show it when he can, but sometimes goes too far.
There is a possibility of listening difficulties.	Listening difficulties can be caused by auditory memory or language comprehension.	Not ready to decide which of the two.
I thought he couldn't remember things that are arbitrary.		For him, memory requires a meaningful context. HE REMEMBERS MANY FACTS THAT ARE MEANINGFULLY EMBEDDED FOR HIM, BUT HAS DIFFICULTY REMEMBERING ARBITRARY OR MEANINGLESS FACTS (STATES, NUMBERS).
	Brief responses can be a value, or language difficulties, or both.	The language hypothesis is consistent with evidence of language LD in Table 6.
He appears limited in expressive language.	Limited expressive language is a sign of language LD.	Additional evidence for language LD.
He is unable to put this sentence together grammatically.		His inability to construct grammatic sentences may have cost him success on some items. HE HAS DIFFICULTY EXPRESSING HIMSELF ON THE LEVEL OF HIS UNDERSTANDING.
	People with grammatic problems often have language LD.	More evidence of language LD to add to above evidence.

(continued)

Table 7 *(Continued)*

Particular information	
Objective observations	Inferred states of mind
	On Picture Arrangement, he was competitive. . . . He was also competitive on Arithmetic.
	[On Picture Arrangement he was] well-oriented and realistic.
	On [the WISC-R] Arithmetic [subtest] he was a good listener.
[He got WISC-R Block Design item 7 wrong. For description of his Block Design behavior, see p. 119.]	*On Block Design, he is not a detail person.*
[*Holistic method* refers to assembling the blocks by intuition; *analytic method* refers to mentally breaking the pattern into squares for the blocks, and arranging the blocks accordingly.]	*When he finally had to switch from the holistic to analytic method, because the items got too difficult to see the answer right away . . .*

Small-sample inductive conclusions that can also serve as particular information	General knowledge	Conclusions
Generalized descriptions	General knowledge	Explanations and higher-order generalizations
He is a competitive person.	Personality characteristics pervade all areas of life.	*He hates special education because [it is like] losing in a game.*
	Realistic but academically weak students fit the model LD picture.	Inconclusive, but consistent with LD.
	Arithmetic is vulnerable to listening problems. Arithmetic questions are more clear-cut than other verbal subtests and might involve less complex language.	*His difficulty isn't listening in itself; it's comprehension of complex language. He doesn't get the long complex sentences.* HE IS AN EXCELLENT LISTENER WHEN THE STIMULUS IS CLEAR-CUT, BUT HAS DIFFICULTY UNDERSTANDING COMPLEX LANGUAGE.
He is holistic. He doesn't analyze.	People with Block Design behavior discussed on p. 119 are holistic in their approach to problems.	Combined with above information, this is fairly conclusive evidence that he is a holistic thinker.
		Combined with above math behavior, *I think he gets too confident, or it isn't "cool" to check.*
	See above.	HIS HOLISTIC (GLOBAL) PERFORMANCE ON HAND–EYE TASKS IS CONSISTENT WITH BEING LEFT-HANDED WITH A HOOKED PENCIL HOLD.

(continued)

Table 7 *(Continued)*

Particular information	
Objective observations	Inferred states of mind
. . . [when] the items got too difficult to see the answer right away, did he a lot of block-turning. . . .	*. . . (trial and error), and finally used an analytic approach on the last item.*
He was persistent on Block Design.	
[He made associations to the relevant facts easily.]	
. . . but had difficulty with language structure. [This refers to responses that are not grammatical, or grammatically parallel to the stimulus word.]	
On Object Assembly, he closed his eyes while the pieces were being put out behind the screen. . . .	
On Comprehension, he offered spontaneous plural responses, sometimes several of them.	

Note. Italicized statements are from the original behavioral notes. Bracketed statements have been reconstructed in search of the basis for entries in other columns on the same row. Capitalized statements are from the final report.

Small-sample inductive conclusions that can also serve as particular information	General knowledge	Conclusions
Generalized descriptions	General knowledge	Explanations and higher-order generalizations
	See above.	LACK OF ANALYSIS AND ATTENTION TO DETAIL IS PARTLY HIS STYLE, AND PARTLY THE RESULT OF OVERCONFIDENCE IN HIS CONSIDERABLE HOLISTIC ABILITIES.
HE IS EXTREMELY COMPETITIVE AND SELF-MOTIVATED ON TASKS HE CAN SUCCEED ON.	Small behaviors reflect larger, more important behavior.	
On Vocabulary, he gave the impression of being very intelligent.		
More evidence of language difficulties.	People with grammatic problems often have language LD.	This is another sample to add to his poorly constructed sentence quoted above.
. . . showing his basic cooperativeness.	Small behaviors reflect larger, more important behavior.	
He did especially well on the more practical items.	Spontaneous plural responses are a sign of above-average ability. People show their ability best in their strongest areas.	HE HAS EXCELLENT PRACTICAL UNDERSTANDING. . . .

Example 4-8

Jason, 10-8, grade 4

Wechsler Intelligence Scale for Children—Revised
(IQ scores 90-109 and scaled scores 8-11 are in the average range. W
shows a subtest significantly weak for its subscale.)

Verbal Tests		Performance Tests	
Information	10	Picture Completion	12
Similarities	8	Picture Arrangement	11
Arithmetic	9	Block Design	11
Vocabulary	9	Object Assembly	13
Comprehension	10	Coding	8 W
(Digit Span)	(7)		
Verbal Scale IQ	95	Performance Scale IQ	106

Full Scale IQ   100

Test Results: Cross-Checking the Evidence

In the individualized interpretation of test scores, the examiner is free to use the subtest equivalencies of Level 1 interpretation and the research-based data of Level 2 *if they fit the case,* but is not bound by them or limited to them. Instead, the scores are treated as hypotheses and cross-checked against all other information.

← In Example 4-8, Jason's test scores, the most important score is generally conceded to be the global one that predicts the person's capacity for schoolwork, if not mental work in general, in this case the IQ of 100. In individualized interpretation, this score is compared with all other known relevant information: his previous IQ score of 120 and his test behavior. The test behavior relevant to global intelligence includes *on Vocabulary, he gave the impression of being very intelligent.* . . . and on *Comprehension, he offered spontaneous plural responses.* His previous score and test behavior converge to cast doubt on the 100 IQ score. Jason seems to have higher potential.

His WISC-R profile shows only one significant score difference as judged by the interpretive rules then in effect, a weakness in Coding. Coding has been linked to a number of abilities (Kaufman, 1979). Several involve general hand–eye skills. Jason's creditable showing on the other performance subtests negates this deficiency. Two abilities that seem relevant are pencil skills and sequential ability. Jason's pencil work seen in Figure 2 (p. 17) is neat and flowing, although the level of the written expression raises a question about the possible role of past difficulty with a pencil in his underachievement. The pencil skills hypothesis is inconclusive. The sequential abilities hypothesis fits with two examination behavioral notes: *He is left-handed with a hooked pencil hold.* Left-handed people, especially with a hooked hold, are supposed to be holistic rather than sequential. On the same theme, *On Block Design, he is not a detail person. He is holistic. He doesn't analyze.*

Negative findings are also findings. The absence of other significant differences should also be validated against other relevant information. The nonsignificance of the Verbal–Performance discrepancy is contradicted by test behaviors: *He appears limited in expressive language. His difficulty . . . [is] comprehension of complex language. On Vocabulary, he . . . had difficulty with language structure.* These behaviors are strong evidence for a language learning disability despite the not-quite-significant difference.

There are also behavioral notes that seem to contradict the absence of subtest scatter by suggesting some disparate separate abilities:

Example 4-8 *(continued)*

Achievements:

Reading:

	Grade Equivalent	Percentile Rank	Standard Score
Decoding: WRAT-R, Level 1	2 Mid.	1	65

Comprehension: New Sucher-Allred Reading Placement Inventory
  Instructional Level: Grade 1
  Frustration Level: Grade 2
  See comments under Discussion below

Written Expression:

	Grade Equivalent	Percentile Rank	Standard Score
Spelling: WRAT-R, Level 1	2 Beg.	2	69

Writing sample, criterion-referenced, using standards from the
    local curriculum
  Capitalization: Inconsistent mastery of first word (grade 1)
  Expression: Beginning grade 3
    Writes and recognizes complete sentence (grade 2+)
    Writes short story in proper sequence (grade 2+)
  Language: Below thought level shown elsewhere (grade 2 to 3)
  Handwriting: Uses cursive script (grade 4)

Math: Criterion-referenced, using examples from the Brigance
  Inventory of Basic Skills, and standards from local curriculum:
  Grade 4, gap at grade 3
    Multidigit subtraction with borrowing (grade 3+)
    Multiplication facts need refreshing (grade 3)
    Multiplies 3 digits × 1 digit with carrying (grade 4)

I thought he couldn't remember things that are arbitrary suggests difficulty with automatic memory. *On Arithmetic he was a good listener. His difficulty isn't listening itself; it's comprehension of complex language.* This suggests adequate memory for meaningful auditory material that is linguistically simple.

His interview responses about interests, identification, and possible heredity suggest strengths as well. *Would like to do the same work as his dad [technical specialty]. Likes to build things with batteries that make light bulbs light.* These suggest above-average holistic hand–eye ability.

← The achievement testing practices illustrated in this book minimize scores in the usual sense, using criterion-referenced rather than norm-referenced tests whenever practical. (See Note 1, Chapter 1; and Chapter 6, pp. 180-181.) The only two norm-referenced scores, Word Recognition and Spelling, show Jason grossly below grade level and expectancy. The criterion-referenced test results, given in whole-grade levels, also show him far below grade level in reading and written expression, the language-related skills affected by language learning disability.

The adequacy of Jason's math achievement shows his normal ability in an area unaffected by language learning disability. Not having mastered the multiplication facts shows his difficulty remembering non-meaningful material, mentioned above.

The Completed Report Revived

Example 4-9 brings back Jason's complete report, this time as the product of reasoning from background information, behavioral notes, and test results. This reasoning process is reflected but not spelled out in the discussion section. (See Chapter 1, p. 15; Chapter 6, p. 182).

Example 4-9

Name: Jason
Age: 10-8
Grade: 4

Reason for Referral: Re-evaluation every 3 years to determine continued eligibility for special services.

Background Information:

Early Development and Medical: Jason's mother was prescribed medication for difficulties during pregnancy. Jason was born in the

(continued)

Example 4-9 *(continued)*

posterior presentation. At 2 years, a fall caused a cut on the forehead, but he did not lose consciousness. At 2½ he had a high fever without convulsions. Developmental milestones were normal.

When Jason was 7-5, an optometrist found normal eyesight, but "multisensory difficulties that made school difficult."

When he was 8-1, a pediatric neurologist diagnosed developmental dyslexia.

Family: Jason and his sister, 12, live with their parents, who are both employed.

Activities, Interests: Jason enjoys playing basketball, baseball, and soccer. He likes to build things with batteries that make light bulbs light.

School History:

In kindergarten, he "needed to work on motor skills." [This usually refers to crayons, pencil, and scissors.] He was coded learning disabled at the end of grade 1 and has remained so ever since. Services have included speech/language. In grade 2, his language-related tool skills were moved to the resource room. He now spends 7.5 hours a week there.

He does especially well on science projects, and just earned an A on one.

Previous Tests:

Age 6-2, at his preschool screening, Jason failed the Preschool Speech and Language Test. The Gesell School Readiness Test found immature fine-motor skills.

Age 7-7, on a WISC-R, Jason scores VSIQ 113, PSIQ 123, and FSIQ 120; with significant strengths in Vocabulary and Mazes, and significant weaknesses in Digit Span and Picture Completion. A speech and language examination at that time showed age-appropriate vocabulary and concepts, but a 1-year lag in language processing and expressive language.

Test Results:

Wechsler Intelligence Scale for Children—Revised
(IQ scores 90-109 and scaled scores 8-11 are in the average range. W shows a subtest significantly weak for its subscale.)

(continued)

Example 4-9 *(continued)*

Verbal Tests		Performance Tests	
Information	10	Picture Completion	12
Similarities	8	Picture Arrangement	11
Arithmetic	9	Block Design	11
Vocabulary	9	Object Assembly	13
Comprehension	10	Coding	8 W
(Digit Span)	(7)		

Verbal Scale IQ	95	Performance Scale IQ	106
	Full Scale IQ	100	

Achievements:

Reading:

	Grade Equivalent	Percentile Rank	Standard Score
Decoding: WRAT-R, Level 1	2 Mid.	1	65

Comprehension: New Sucher-Allred Reading Placement Inventory
   Instructional Level: Grade 1
   Frustration Level: Grade 2
   See comments under <u>Discussion</u> below

Written Expression:

Spelling: WRAT-R, Level 1	2 Beg.	2	69

Writing sample, criterion-referenced, using standards from the
      local curriculum
   Capitalization: Inconsistent mastery of first word
      (grade 1)
   Expression: Beginning grade 3
      Writes and recognizes complete sentence (grade 2+)
      Writes short story in proper sequence (grade 2+)
      Language: Below thought level shown elsewhere (grade 2 to 3)
      Handwriting: Uses cursive script (grade 4)

Math: Criterion-referenced, using examples from the Brigance
   Inventory of Basic Skills, and standards from local curriculum:
   Grade 4, gap at grade 3
      Multidigit subtraction with borrowing (grade 3+)
      Multiplication facts need refreshing (grade 3)
      Multiplies 3 digits × 1 digit with carrying (grade 4)

(continued)

Example 4-9 *(continued)*

Discussion:

Jason is at least 5 feet tall, mature, well-oriented, realistic, and attentive. He dislikes needing special services, and felt negative about being tested, but nevertheless cooperated thoroughly. He is extremely competitive and self-motivated on tasks he can succeed on.

Although the only significantly weak WISC-R subtest score is Coding, Jason's behavior showed many learning discrepancies. He is an excellent listener when the stimulus is clear-cut, but has difficulty understanding complex language. He remembers many facts that are meaningfully embedded for him, but has difficulty remembering arbitrary or meaningless facts (states, numbers). He has excellent practical understanding, but has difficulty expressing himself in language on the level of his understanding. His holistic (global) performance on hand–eye tasks is consistent with being left-handed with a hooked pencil hold. Lack of analysis and attention to detail is partly his style, and partly the result of overconfidence in his considerable holistic abilities. Jason's many learning disabilities, most of which do not show up in the test profile, and the quality of some of his responses, suggest that he is brighter than his present IQ scores show. The drop in scores since his last test often accompanies a learning disability, as the test content becomes increasingly school-influenced with age.

Decoding is a serious problem for Jason. He missequences sounds on some one-syllable words *(felt)*, and has difficulty with two-syllable words. He says he has enjoyed reading sports books. Reading comprehension is severely limited by decoding. He shows excellent comprehension, and high goals in making up titles that summarize the story, on a grade 3 level; but inability to decode key words caused him to fail to answer a passing number of comprehension questions above the grade 1 level.

Written expression is affected by oral language expression difficulties. His holistic style is not compatible with being a good speller.

Summary: Jason is a bright boy who is a successful math and science student, a strong thinker, self-motivated where he can succeed, and may be creative; but he has a language-based learning disability, with difficulties in comprehension of complex language and in oral expression on his thought level. In addition, his holistic learning style, which is an asset in mechanics and science, causes difficulty in sequential processes in reading and spelling. His strengths have obscured his learning disabilities in the present WISC-R profile. He is underachieving 3 years in language-related tool skills.

The Psychological Process

When the major part of the data immediately points to unambiguous conclusions, clinical inference follows a convergent, mechanical, information-processing model (p. 77). The more familiar the clinical picture, and the more pictures with which the clinician is familiar, the more cases can be solved this way. But this model does not fit unfamiliar or conflicting data. That calls for a divergent, creative problem-solving model (pp. 77-78).

Incubation

Many people have had the experience of incubation: An elusive piece of information, or the answer to a question or problem, pops into their heads later at an unexpected moment. (See *Incubation and Illumination in Science and Literature*, p. 139.) Incubation can also be a less sudden and dramatic process, whereby situations look different a few days afterward because the relative importance of different aspects of the situation has become clearer.

The incubation period allows a broad search of the human databank for associations and connections, or series of them, not previously considered relevant. The incubation period also allows cross-checking multiple connections with each other, toward a unified picture that takes account of all the data.

Incubation is controversial because not everyone has had the experience. Like dreaming in color, as opposed to black-and-white, those who do not do it have difficulty believing that it happens at all.

Here is an example of an especially obscure association retrieved by incubation in a personality assessment.

> One characteristic of a Rorschach record is the emotional tone. It is not a category in any of the scoring systems, but is nevertheless an important quality to consider.

> Lisa, 13, said in response to Card VII, that it is a person holding the hand—so. She made a gesture with her right hand not easily described, so I sketched a picture of it next to her answer (see Figure 7). She could not explain. But a gesture must have a meaning, even if unintended.

> A few days later I remembered seeing the gesture in classical paintings of biblical figures; it was associated with religious or spiritual qualities. But Lisa came by the symbol much closer to home. A drive past the church in the nearby town found the same gesture on the statue of St. Joseph, the good step-parent.

No computer databank of Rorschach responses would include pictorial associations, or Renaissance art; but incubation can access this material in the latent human databank.

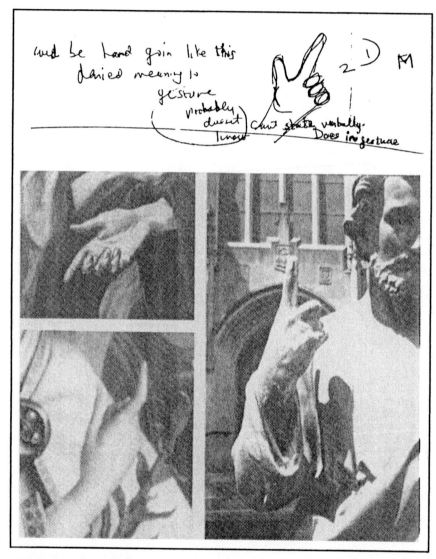

Figure 7. A subject's hand gesture. Top—Sketch of the gesture from Rorschach protocol. Middle left—Detail from El Greco, *St. Peter and St. Paul.* Lower left—Detail from Van Eyck, *The Annunciation.* Lower right— Statue outside church in nearby town.

Disadvantages of incubation. Incubation is probably *not a universal human aptitude*. Some people make all the associations in their repertoire immediately. They either know right away, or they do

---

Incubation and Illumination in Science and Literature

Archimedes Discovers the Law of Displacement of Water

. . . Hiero, after gaining the royal power in Syracuse, resolved . . . to place in a certain temple a golden crown which he had vowed to the immortal gods. He contracted for its making . . . and weighed out a precise amount of gold to the contractor. At the appointed time the latter delivered to the king's satisfaction an exquisitely finished piece of handiwork, and it appeared that in weight the crown corresponded precisely to what the gold had weighed.

But afterwards a charge was made that the gold had been abstracted and an equivalent weight of silver had been added to the manufacture of the crown. Hiero, thinking it an outrage that he had been tricked, but not knowing how to detect the theft, requested Archimedes to consider the matter. The latter, while the case was still on his mind, happened to go to the bath, and on getting into a tub observed that the more his body sank into it the more water ran out over the tub. As this pointed out the way to explain the case in question, without a moment's delay, and transported with joy, he jumped out of the tub and rushed home naked, crying with a loud voice that he had found what he was seeking; for as he ran he shouted repeatedly in Greek, "Eureka, eureka" ["I found it, I found it"].

— Vitruvius

If only I could wake in the morning,
And find I had learned the solution,
Wake with the knack of knowledge
Who as yet have only an inkling.
From "Leaving Barra"
by Louis MacNeice[a]

---

not know at all. The world needs their clear-eyed certainty as well as incubation. *Vive la différence!*

Incubation is *not under complete voluntary control.* Some people cannot tolerate any abdication of control. Even for those who can, incubation can get out of hand. It can wake problem-solvers at 3 a.m., send them reaching for the bedside notepad, and keep them up till 5. Incubation makes writers.

Harnessing the winged horse. It is not possible, by definition, to offer unfailing directions for divergent processes. However, these suggestions are offered for stimulating incubation. It is not enough merely to let time pass. Set the selective focus by reviewing the problem and the data. Then disengage the focus. Sleep on it, or switch to routine or recreational activity, or at least other work. Give incubation reasonable time, at least overnight, but not long enough to forget — perhaps a week at most.

Just as connections available by mechanical processes are immediate, so immediate inferences tend to be mechanically processed: *This*, therefore *that.* When the convergent, mechanical information-processing model is used for problems it does not fit — unfamiliar or conflicting data — the result is inadequate, mechanical interpretation, as shown in Chapter 1, pp. 8-11.

Clinical inference is more complex than finding a connection between a piece of data and knowledge. There is always a multiplicity of data, among problem, background, test scores, and test behavior, necessitating cross-checking and weighing the relative importance of different puzzle pieces. Most cases involve some element of problem solving. Therefore it is best not to write the report on the day of the examination. It is ideal to score the tests and review the data in advance of sitting down to write.

Individual Characteristics That Predispose Some People Toward Clinical Inference

Some people have a greater propensity than others for clinical inference. These are some of the qualities that contribute:

1. An appropriate background of knowledge in the field.
2. Willingness to submit clinical insights to the discipline of cross-checking.
3. A tendency to see things in wholes rather than in parts.[14]
4. Field independence in problem solving (see Note 14).

5. Freedom from personal investment in the outcome of the examination.

Professional education addresses acquiring knowledge and intellectual discipline, but my impression has been that it discourages holistic and field-independent students, or at best does nothing to encourage them.

Personal investment might result from interest in demonstrating particular theories or disorders because they are of professional or personal interest to the examiner, or because they are in style and confer respect on those who invoke them. Personal investment also results from the need for conclusions desired by those paying for the examination. Adversarial testing, as in contested cases, is not geared to reaching unbiased conclusions and ultimately works to the detriment of the profession that offers itself for hire.

DEMONSTRATION OR CLINICAL PROOF

Cross-Checking the Evidence

Use of the criteria of a theory (pp. 80-82) to decide between two competing hypotheses is demonstrated with faithful subject Jason.

The hypothesis based on Jason's WISC-R scores alone (see the Level 2 interpretation, Chapter 1, pp. 8-11) is that he is not learning disabled. His profile is fairly flat, with no "peaks and valleys." A barely significant weakness in Coding suggests possible pencil difficulties; even this significance is retracted by the revision of Kaufman's Practitioners' Rules, Chapter 1, p. 9.

The hypothesis based on his learning-related test behavior (see the Level 3 interpretation, Chapter 1, pp. 12-20, and the present chapter, pp. 120-133) is that he *is* a learning-disabled student, with receptive and expressive language difficulties, whose global learning style hinders sequential activities like decoding and spelling.

The first criterion of a theory is *comprehensiveness,* fitting the facts of the case. The Level 2 interpretation fits the WISC-R, but it does not fit the achievement scores or the nonquantitative data—test behavior, school history, and background information. The Level 3 interpretation fits these facts.

The second criterion is *logical consistency.* It must make sense. The referral question is whether or not Jason still has a learning disability. The Level 2 answer is that he probably does not. This does not make a great deal of sense in view of his continuing underachievement in several areas, at least without offering some other explanation for the cause of the discrepancy.

The Test of Time

The third criterion, *predictive ability,* would be seen if other specialists tested Jason. The speech and language examination of a language learning–disabled student would be expected to show difficulties. Predictive ability would be seen eventually in his next 3-year update examination. This is *the test of time.*

Time tests previous tests. Although new referrals cannot wait for the proof of time, every re-evaluation puts previous examinations to time's test.

The scores from Jason's previous test, age 7-7, do not have much in common with his present scores. Almost the only results in common are serious underachievement in reading, and eligibility for a learning disabilities coding. The most prophetic information in his file is a speech and language examination from about the same time, which found vocabulary and concepts age-appropriate, but a 1-year lag in language processing and expressive language. The report does not tell where this placed him in comparison with population norms, but is suggestive of the present picture. The 20-point drop in IQ score says a great deal about how much learning disabilities hold children back in comparison with their peers.

The verdict of time about Jason's present examination will be seen from whether his special program helps him make reasonably steady progress in his low areas, whether he succeeds as a junior and senior high school math and science student, and perhaps whether he eventually attends a college or technical institute.

Just before this book went to press, the writer had the opportunity to administer the test of time by giving Jason's *next* 3-year evaluation.

Jason was now 13-7. The new WISC-R scores are Verbal Scale IQ 103, Performance Scale IQ 115, and Full Scale IQ 109. The test of time supports the language learning disability hypothesis with a significant Verbal–Performance discrepancy, and confirms the impression of above-average ability by the Performance score. A significantly weak Coding score supports the hypothesis of a holistic person who is weaker at sequential tasks. A significantly strong Arithmetic subtest shows the competitive fledgling engineer secure on his own turf. Learning-related test behavior shows that Jason no longer relies on intuition; he solved both spatial and academic problems methodically, using analysis and utilizing detail. His achievements are now within the average range, showing the results of his ability and motivation, an appropriate school program, and parental support. For the past 2 years, resource room time has been minimal with an element of choice. His teachers see him as a college-bound student, and he is on the basketball team.

Occam's Razor and Factor Scores

The first three criteria for judging hypotheses favor the Level 3 interpretation of Jason's original examination over the Level 2 interpretation so decisively that the tie-breaker criterion of *simplicity* need not be used.

Factor Scores

Occam's Razor is, however, relevant to the use of *factor scores,* which are a refinement of mechanical (Level 2) interpretation. Factor scores are calculated by averaging the subtests that make up each factor (see p. 52). These factor scores are compared with the subject's average scaled score, and a test of significance used to identify strong or weak factors.

Various factors in Wechsler's tests have been identified, some by armchair analysis and some by empirical research. Kaufman (1979, pp. 134-171) presents a fairly exhaustive list of 34 "patterns" that others have used to derive factor scores.

Obtaining factor scores, however, is not enough. One unusually high or low score can unduly influence the average. There must also be a test for whether the factors "hold together" — whether they are really factors at all in the case under consideration. There is a statistical formula for this decision as well.

A number of computer programs are available that extract various sets of factors from Wechsler profiles. I reviewed five computerized interpretations of Jason's original test profile. None revealed any significant strengths or weaknesses.

One of these programs (*Dumont/Faro,* 1989), originally consisting of 33 factors, has since been revised with the addition of another list of 39 factors (*Dumont/Faro,* 1990, see Note 15). About half the new factors duplicate some of the original 33, but some are calculated by a different method, with a resulting unduplicated list of 55 factors. This expanded list turned out to be more powerful than its predecessor. It found 4 strong factors (*perceptual organization, spatial, nonverbal reasoning,* and *trial-and-error*) and 4 weak ones (*freedom from distractibility, sequential, fund of information,* and *verbal reasoning*).

The power of this revised program consists of its having found some significant factors where other programs did not. But are they the right ones?

The overlapping strong factors *perceptual organization, spatial,* and *nonverbal* fit Jason at age 10. *Trial-and-error* does not. Jason solves problems by intuitive leaps. When this fails, he is not very successful at trial-and-error because he does not learn from his errors. Two of the weak factors fit Jason, *sequential* and *fund of information,* which tends to be low in underachieving students. But he is not particularly *distractible,* although he is impulsive, which goes with distractibility. It is Jason's language expression that is weak rather than his *verbal reasoning,* which is adequate when allowances are made for his expressive language difficulties. Of 8 significant factors out of 55, 5 fit Jason and 3 do not.

The drawback to these findings is that the significant factors only partially match the behavior they are supposed to reflect. The case of Ricky, Chapter 5, pp. 154-159, is an example of contradiction between a factor score and behavior.

There is a potential statistical difficulty with using a list of factors as long as this program. If computing 55 factors yields 8 significant ones, there are questions as to (1) whether the test of significance used takes the large number of comparisons into account, and (2) whether close to 8 factors would turn up for almost any subject, LD or not. The latter is the same problem as the too many tests problem (pp. 95-97).

But the greatest drawback to factor scores is not with the factors themselves but with the examiners: Many do not bother to cross-check the scores against evidence from other sources. Factor scores are only meant to be hypotheses, but some examiners accept them as unquestioned truth. From the computer's mathematical precision, they jump to believing in its logical truth, which it does not have the data or the categories to justify.

Are Factor Scores Simpler than Individualized Interpretation?

There are two ways that the factor scores method differs from the method of comparing subtest scores used in individualized interpretation: (1) Computing factor scores is a *precise* mathematical procedure, whereas inspecting, or looking at, subtest scores involves a more *informal* comparison. (2) Factor scores are a *deductive* method (p. 72) that begins with the factors to be derived from the scores—a pattern to impose on them. The individualized method is *inductive* (pp. 72-75). It begins with the subject's scores: Look to see if any are significantly high or low, or if any lean in that direction. Recall, or figure out, the possible interpretations of those subtests, either separately or in combination. Then cross-check these tentative interpretations against test behavior.

Inspecting subtest scores and recalling or reasoning out interpretive hypotheses to check against behavioral observation is simpler than computing 55, or even 39, factors and determining whether each is unitary. The fact that someone (or something) else does the computation does not make the process simpler. It only shifts the responsibility.

However, there is an assumption behind the use of inductive reasoning. The examiner must have some knowledge of different possible meanings of subtest scores, or the ability to figure them out. Some examiners have little faith in their knowledge and reasoning.

There is also a strong element of individual taste in this choice. Some people feel more comfortable with a mathematical-deductive approach, whereas others prefer a greater component of experience. I believe Occam favors inductive reasoning from inspection of scores, over computation of factor scores.

BEYOND THE REFERRAL QUESTION:
THE PRACTITIONER'S RESPONSIBILITY

Jason's special program is addressing his learning problem. But what of the boy behind the problem — the boy who likes active sports, and builds things with batteries that make light bulbs light and earned an A on a science project?

Special education machinery tends to grind on, remediating weaknesses, and paying little attention to talents, or to the student as a person with needs beyond academic remediation. Remediation is never the whole picture. The examiner is often the only person whose role it is to look at the entire situation. Examiners should affirm this role and speak up for the person behind the problem.

The recommendations of a report often get particular attention. After recommendations for Jason about services, methods, and materials, some recommendations were addressed to athlete-engineer Jason, and to the parents who worried enough to take him to an optometrist and a pediatric neurologist.

Example 4-10

Recommendations:

Jason needs continued success and reinforcement in his strong areas: science, math, and athletics.

(continued)

Example 4-10 *(continued)*

Home construction activities are a plus. They should be utilized in school as much as possible. He might have an opportunity to bring home projects to school, and to participate in similar ones at school.

Students like Jason sometimes go on to appropriate postsecondary education.

Example 4-11 shows how a solution to the referral question can sometimes work against optimal personal development.

Example 4-11

[16-10, grade 10]

The juvenile court placed this student on probation for truancy. She had missed a great deal of her first year of high school through unexcused absences. The court requested an evaluation for learning disabilities, to see whether learning problems were causing her to avoid school.

Her WAIS-R Full Scale IQ was 89. The profile was unremarkable, with one significantly low score on Picture Arrangement. Her estimated expected achievement level was grade 8, and she was achieving up to her expectancy, or reasonably close to it.

Her account of her lifelong personal adjustment was that she had always been shy and had few friends. She had been interested in some school activities, but had never participated. In junior high school, she sometimes stayed home from school with her mother and watched television.

At the large high school in a nearby city where her town tuitioned its students, she found a social group available to her for the first time. She missed many classes socializing with them in the school cafeteria and courtyard. Her lack of social experience, consistent with her low Picture Arrangement score, kept her from recognizing the unsuitability of her new companions. At the same time her mother discovered her new friends, her guidance counselor pinpointed her attendance problem, and she was placed on probation.

At the time of the evaluation, she had gotten a job after school, and acquired a boyfriend at work who was a high school graduate. She was attending school regularly, and was not having any problems at home or at school.

(continued)

Example 4-11 *(continued)*

The school psychologist was not satisfied with this state of affairs, but raised the issue of social development. The student had never completed the adolescent stage of social group membership, but had stumbled over this issue by choosing the wrong group and getting in trouble with the law. Her response was to retreat from adolescent social life into premature adulthood with job and boyfriend. Her escape from adolescent problems into adulthood skipped the development of important social skills, *even though it helped solve the referral problem.*

The school psychologist recommended that she join a school club for students interested in her favorite vocational subject.

5 INDIVIDUALIZED TEST INTERPRETATION: ONE MORE TEST AND FIVE MORE CASES

This chapter applies individualized interpretation to a greater range of situations: a test of visual perception, a test-of-choice that turns out not to answer the referral question, and some issues of the day—attention deficit and cultural influences in testing.

A TEST OF VISUAL-PERCEPTUAL SKILLS

Examiners have their own repertoires of favorite tests, and the tests cited have reflected the writer's usage. But examiners hear and read other examiners' reports and learn from them.

Praxis, the occupational therapist, combined clinical with statistical reasoning in interpreting a test from her examination of a student named Carlos, age 11-4.

Gardner Test of Visual Perceptual Skills

	Scaled Score	Age Equivalent	Percentile Rank
Visual Discrimination	12	>12-11	75
Visual Memory	9	9- 7	37
Visual Spatial Relations	13	>12-11	84
Visual Form Constancy	7	7- 6	16
Visual Sequential Memory	11	11- 1	63
Visual Figure Ground	6	6-11	9
Visual Closure	8	8- 2	25

Praxis concluded that Carlos' areas of difficulty were *memory,* form constancy, figure ground, and closure. I objected, "But he scored average on two visual memory subtests."

Praxis explained that she based that conclusion on test behavior. Although Carlos achieved an average score on sequential memory, he did this by using a compensatory strategy: He discovered the patterns by counting instead of using his vision. Furthermore, during several subtests he wanted to augment his vision by tracing the design with his finger. This led her to conclude that Carlos had difficulty discriminating what he is looking *at* and therefore also remembering what he is looking *for.* This was slowing down his classroom symbol recognition and copying.

Her conclusion was based on his relatively low scores on several other subtests *and* his behavior in attempting to compensate by two different means on several subtests. Praxis also used her understanding of how the abilities shown on the test are related to classroom learning tasks to specify which tasks were being slowed down.

WHEN THE TEST CATEGORIES DON'T ANSWER THE QUESTION: SCOTT

Name: Scott
Age: 6-0
Grade: Kindergarten

Reason for Referral: Scott is very slow to respond to instruction, and is having difficulty learning.

. . . .

Previous Tests: On the Gesell School Readiness Test, age 5-1, Scott's behaviors ranged from age 3½ to 5, and clustered 4½ to 5. He had difficulty with language and pencil skills.

Test Results:

Stanford-Binet Intelligence Scale: 4th edition
(Scores 89–110 are in the average range, 79–88 in the low average range, and 68–78 in the slow learner range.)

(continued)

Scott *(continued)*

Verbal Reasoning		Quantitative Reasoning Area
Vocabulary	88	See <u>Discussion</u> below
Comprehension	88	
Verbal Reasoning Area	87	

Abstract/Visual Reasoning		Short-Term Memory	
Pattern Analysis	90	Bead Memory	92
Copying	72	Memory for Sentences	78
Abstract/Visual Reasoning Area	78	Short-Term Memory Area	82

Partial Test Composite   79
(Quantitative Reasoning Area omitted)

Draw-A-Person (Goodenough-Harris norms)   86
(Scores 90–109 are in the average range, 80–89 in the low average range.)
   Concept is above level of pencil coordination and spacing

Achievements:

Preacademic concepts:
   Colors: Named red, blue, green, purple, orange
      Did not name yellow, black, white, brown (preschool level)
   Shapes: Named circle and square (preschool level)
   Sequencing pictures: Sequenced 1 of 2 sets correctly
      (developing kindergarten skills)
   Sorting: Sorted into 2 groups by color, shape, and size
   Concepts: Had difficulty with *similarity*

Prereading: Did not name letters (beginning kindergarten)

Prewriting:
   Pencil grip effortful
   Developing ability to copy square on 5-year level

Premath:
   Counted by rote to 30, omitting 16 (kindergarten level)
   Named numbers to 12, except 7 (middle kindergarten)
   Wrote numbers from dictation: 0, 1, 3 (beginning kindergarten)
   Counted objects one-to-one (end kindergarten)
   Concepts: Gave incorrect answer without counting (beginning
      kindergarten)

(continued)

Scott *(continued)*

Discussion:

Scott is a tall, good-looking boy who initially expressed anxiety by squinting and grimacing, but soon settled down and became calm, trusting, and affectionate. He has immature speech sound substitutions, and he answered many questions in the prelogical manner of a preschool child. He indicated that he finds many kindergarten activities frustrating. He prefers blocks, and his own toys brought from home.

His general youngness affected his test performance in many ways. He does not leave himself a clear workspace. He has difficulty following directions. He has not acquired some concepts needed on the Binet, most notably, *like.*

The Quantitative Reasoning Area score was originally low (64) because it requires the concept *like.* I tested limits for this area by explaining *like* and readministering. He scored average (98). This area is therefore not included in the Test Composite.

Scott shows a difference between language and spatial abilities, which is hidden in the area and subtest scores. The Verbal Reasoning Area, at his age level, is less demanding of language concepts than the Quantitative Area or, for that matter, than the interview. He is solidly average on the Pattern Analysis subtest, which is similar to the WISC-R Block Design; and he showed ability to criticize his performance. He is also average in visual memory (Bead Memory subtest), despite missing some easy items that did not capture his interest. Although he scored lower on Copying (a less structured task using solid color blocks) than on Pattern Analysis, he did good work on Copying both in reproducing patterns and in fine-motor coordination; but reversals lowered his score.

Summary: Scott tests in the Low Average range. However, average scores and qualitatively good performance on spatial tasks, and lack of some needed language concepts, raise the possibility of a language deficit in comprehension, concepts, and expression.

There are two difficulties in interpreting Scott's Stanford-Binet IV scores. The Binet IV areas—Verbal Reasoning, Abstract/Visual Reasoning, Quantitative Reasoning, and Short-Term Memory—do not make distinctions about Scott that explain his school difficulties. Furthermore, some scores are in disagreement with important test behavior.

Scott's highest area score, Verbal Reasoning, is his lowest area of behavior: *has difficulty following directions, answered many questions in the prelogical manner of a preschool child.* The Quantitative Reasoning Area score was invalidated by Scott's lack of the language concept *like*; for him the quantitative items were a verbal reasoning task. *Immature speech sound substitutions* are not necessarily relevant, as many children with excellent language have these, but pronunciation difficulties could be an aspect of immature language development. Difficulty in language on the Gesell 1 year earlier is additional supporting evidence that this is a low area. The close-to-average Verbal Reasoning score might be explained on the grounds that the Vocabulary and Comprehension subtests that comprise this area are easier for Scott than following directions, answering open-ended interview questions, and understanding relational concepts. The Binet subtest items are more focused, come in repetitive sets, and at this age level have briefer questions and more automatic responses.

In Scott's Binet profile, as often happens, the differences between subtests *within* areas are more striking than the differences *between* areas, suggesting that the examiner should recategorize the subtests into groupings that make more sense for this child. Sattler's (1988, pp. 257-259) suggested Binet IV factors—at Scott's age, a verbal and a nonverbal factor—are one possibility. I prefer a more inductive approach, looking at each child's higher and lower subtests and seeing what they have in common, but always also cross-checking with behavior for subtest meanings different from their given names. Scott's higher scores besides the verbal ones are Bead Memory and Pattern Analysis. Checking these scores against behavior, Pattern Analysis is *solidly* [connotes little internal scatter, a sign of reliability] *average . . . and he showed ability to criticize his performance,* showing that he is more advanced on this task than the prelogical stage of his language. Bead Memory is *average . . . despite missing some easy items that did not capture his interest,* suggesting that his score is minimal, and was lowered by immature behavior, not settling right down to business.

Both strong subtests are in the nonverbal area. Looking to see how the other nonverbal subtest, Copying, fits with these, this subtest also shows good nonverbal ability in both perceptual and motor aspects, *did good work . . . both in reproducing patterns and in fine-motor coordination.* Copying, however, was lowered even more than Bead Memory, by a behavior that at this age might be considered primarily immaturity: *reversals lowered his score.*

The low Memory for Sentences subtest score is consistent with both his language behavior, *difficulty following directions,* and immaturity, *his general youngness.*

Scott's pattern of abilities seems made for the WISC-R categories, Verbal and Performance. His age, however, is 6-0, the young edge of the WISC-R range. A child this young who does not do well on the WISC-R may get some raw scores of zero, which invalidate the test. At this age, even raw scores above zero may represent very few responses, so that the scaled scores are not based on much information. Statistical standardization does not make up for this weak foundation.

The Stanford-Binet, extending downward to age 2-0, gives Scott the opportunity to show an ample range of behaviors establishing a basal level. Better to give a test with a solid foundation at the child's age level, and use the more complete information it provides to sort the data into the categories that best fit the child in view of the whole picture.

ATTENTION DEFICIT: RICKY AND TODD

Ricky: The Distractibility Factor Fails to Discriminate

One of the clichés of Wechsler pattern interpretation is that attention deficit is recognizable from the Third Factor, weakness in a triad of subtests, Arithmetic, Digit Span, and Coding.[1] Many persons with attention deficit do indeed score low on one or more of these subtests. The Wechsler tests, however, were not designed to diagnose attention deficit; and there are several instruments designed to do so, that do it much better.

Name: Ricky
Age: 8-9
Grade: 2

Reason for Referral: Ricky has a great deal of difficulty with academic work. He works hard, but distractibility and disorganization are problems.

. . . .

Test Results:

Wechsler Intelligence Scale for Children — Revised
(IQ scores 90–109 and scaled scores 8–11 are in the average range. IQ scores 80–89 and scaled scores 7 are in the low average range. Scaled

(continued)

Ricky *(continued)*

scores 14 are superior, and 5 are deficient. S and W show subtests significantly strong or weak for their subscale.)

Verbal Tests		Performance Tests	
Information	8	Picture Completion	10
Similarities	7	Picture Arrangement	14 (S)
Arithmetic	9	Block Design	10
Vocabulary	8	Object Assembly	10
Comprehension	8	Coding	5 (W)
(Digit Span)	(11)		

Verbal Scale IQ   87   Performance Scale IQ 98

Full Scale IQ   97

*Median Test Age   8-2

*Mean Test Age could not be computed because Ricky scored below the norms on one subtest.

Bender Visual Motor Gestalt
Gets the perceptual gestalt
Drawings are simplified, and show lack of precision and
impulsivity that increases with difficulty
Memory: Intermediate grades level

Achievements:

	Grade Equivalent	Percentile Rank	Standard Score
Reading:			
Decoding: WRAT-R, Level 1	1 End	3	72

Comprehension:
Could not handle Primer Level of New Sucher-Allred Reading
Placement Inventory
Gates-MacGinitie Reading Tests, Primary A 1.7
(probably inflated)

Written Expression:

	Grade Equivalent	Percentile Rank	Standard Score
Spelling: WRAT-R, Level 1	2 Middle	7	78

Writing Sample, criterion-referenced, using standards from the
local curriculum: Developing grade-appropriate skills
Handwriting: Large

(continued)

Ricky *(continued)*

Capitalization: Grade 2, gap at grade 1
  I, first word of sentence (1st +)
  Some extraneous capitals (1st)
  Proper nouns (2nd)
Punctuation: Grade 2
  Period in sentence (1st +), abbreviations (2nd)
  Question mark (2nd)
  Does not use comma in date (Beginning 2nd)
Expression: End grade 1 to beginning grade 2
  Sentence: Writes 6-word sentence based on thought
  Paragraph: Does not write more than one sentence

Math: Beginning grade 2

  Addition: Sums to 10 automatic, to 20 on fingers
  Subtraction: Uses fingers
  Experience: Says he plays cards

Discussion:

Ricky is a positive, spontaneous boy who is large for his age, let alone his class. He showed a happy, self-protective disposition, doing his best, taking an easier route or declining a task if necessary, and accepting the resulting work and himself. His language is not school-like, but communicates well and sometimes has a dramatic flair. He sometimes remembered important facts but not the associated names, or remembered a word similar to the right one but not precisely correct.

At the beginning, he paid excellent attention, focused and followed directions well, and thought out language problems. After about 20 minutes, however, he became physically restless; after an hour, stood up; and by 1½ hours was walking around, despite three breaks. Restlessness and frustration were expressed by overflow ("Boo-boo-boo-boo"), making comments to himself, and speaking in a singsong tone. Impulsivity was most apparent on hand–eye tasks. Disorganization showed in inability to eat his snack and do any work at the same time.

. . . .

Summary: . . . Impulsivity, heightened by fatigue and frustration, compounds his difficulties. . . .

Ricky's verbal subtests do not reflect any ill effects of distractibility. All are in the average or low average range. Those involving numbers are slightly and nonsignificantly higher. This slight difference might be meaningful in view of his math being much closer to grade level than reading and written expression and his saying that he plays cards. It is midyear, and many in his class have mastered addition and subtraction facts to 18, but he has not. Because memory is quite adequate (Digit Span score 11), the problem seems to be not getting down to work, *taking an easier route and declining a task if necessary*. Impulsive children often enjoy computers (the button-pushing-menace factor), and he might find a computer math facts program motivating.

Good memory for numbers does not extend to words. *He is apt to remember important facts but forget the associated names, or remember a word that is similar but not precisely the right one*. He might have a word-retrieval problem. That diagnosis is the speech/language specialist's turf.

The first four performance subtests, the Perceptual Organization factor, is strong average. Above-average, significantly strong Picture Arrangement is often associated with social understanding. This is consistent with *communicates well*. The significantly weak Coding score has a number of possible meanings. Three are pencil skills, short-term visual memory, and distractibility.

Difficulty with pencil skills is consistent with *large handwriting,* and *does not write more than one sentence* when the children in his class are writing stories. The short-term visual memory hypothesis is contradicted by Ricky's memory for the Bender designs. He drew five from memory after the regular administration, the standard for the intermediate grades (4 to 6), according to a criterion of unknown origin once passed along by some long-gone colleague. The distractibility hypothesis is consistent with Ricky's behavior and Bender Gestalt (discussed below). The same distractibility has not lowered the other two subtests in the Third Factor, as *impulsivity was most apparent on hand–eye tasks*. This observation refers to all the performance subtests, but the first four are simultaneous tasks and therefore less vulnerable.

Figure 8 shows Ricky's Bender Gestalt protocol. Ricky has captured the gestalt (configuration) of each design fairly accurately, with no rotations or serious distortions. Coordination is fairly good on the larger shapes. Lines are moderately straight, curves regular, and many angles well-joined. It is in the small design-units that the difficulty shows.

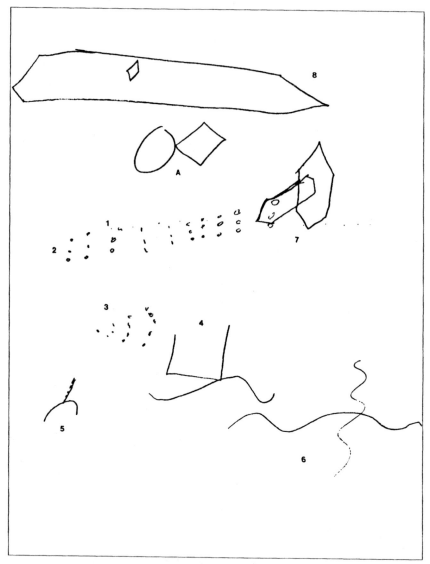

Figure 8.   Ricky's Bender protocol.

Large handwriting. Difficulty making small pencil-shapes interacts with impulsivity, *most apparent on hand–eye tasks,* in his protocol.

Design A is quite accurate except for the failure to close the circle. Because he joins more difficult forms, this closure is within his ability, and the omission is due to hurry, lack of attention to detail, impulsivity. He forms the dots in design 1 by jabbing the pencil-point on the paper instead of attempting the more controlled act of drawing, a combination of knowing the task is difficult for him and *taking an easier route.* On design 2 he begins by neglecting to consider spacing, so that design 2 covers design 1. The three small circles in the first three rows approach adequacy for his age, but the rows slant the wrong way. To improve the slant, he must simplify the circles to dots, which in his impulsive style become slashes. After two successfully slanted rows of dot-slashes, he tries to achieve a row of circles correctly slanted. He almost achieves one row — one of the circles is a semi-circle — but cannot keep it up, and his rows of circles revert to the old slant and become larger and farther apart, expansive and impulsive.

Design 3 shows the same conflict between perception and pencil coordination. He can either preserve the gestalt or make correct small forms (in this case dots), but not both at once. Design 4 is too close to design 3, and getting larger. Design 5 is smaller because it is difficult for him, and shows the breakdown in efforts at control as he gives up on dots and regresses to the linear form that is on the 4-year level. Design 6 is even closer to 4 and larger, and runs off the page. The difficulty of design 7 decreases the size again, and forces him to pay closer attention to drawing, but in doing so, he loses sight of the relationship to the other drawings, and draws on top of another design. Design 8 continues the trend of increasing size and almost runs off the page.

Throughout the Bender, Ricky has difficulty with pencil coordination on the small forms; responds to difficulty by retrenching (decreasing the size), regressing, and making errors of (spatial) judgment; and responds generally by increasing impulsivity and expansiveness.

Impulsivity is also his outstanding behavioral characteristic observed during testing. He is a well-intentioned boy, *at the beginning he paid excellent attention, focused and followed directions well,* but he cannot maintain this attention; and, his inattention has a great many physical accompaniments described in the second paragraph of the discussion section of the report.

Ricky's factor scores from the three-factor model (Cohen, 1952, 1957, 1959) are

Verbal Comprehension	7.5
Perceptual Organization	11
Freedom from Distractibility	8.33

This sytem does not find Ricky's Third Factor comparatively low. However, the hypothesized meaning of this factor does not fit the facts of this case — the impulsivity so clearly present in his behavior and the Bender Gestalt.

Todd: Attention Deficit Muddies the Water

Mariana, the resource room teacher and school coordinator of referrals, asked what to do about her new pupil, Todd, who was coming to her for help on a trial basis. Charlotte Hollister had tested him privately just before the school year began. The WISC-R profile did not signify any learning disabilities, but Dr. Hollister nevertheless felt that Todd had some and wanted the school district to do more testing to find them. Dr. Hollister also tested for longstanding behavioral and attentional problems. His mother had not liked Todd's response to medication. He was responding well to Mariana's behavior management techniques, but was not transferring this improvement to his regular classroom. He was learning in the resource room, but not performing in the classroom. Was anything to be gained from testing Todd?

Name: Todd
Age: 6-8
Grade: 1
Examiner: Charlotte Hollister

Test Results: Wechsler Intelligence Scale for Children — Revised

Verbal Tests		Performance Tests	
Information	7	Picture Completion	10
Similarities	6 (W)	Picture Arrangement	9
Arithmetic	10	Block Design	7
Vocabulary	9	Object Assembly	10
Comprehension	13 (S)	Coding	8
(Digit Span)	(8)		

Verbal Scale IQ   94   Performance Scale IQ   91

Full Scale IQ   91

Owens Attention Deficit Disorder Behavioral Rating Scale:
Parent and teacher responded to this scale. Both saw Todd as inattentive and having difficulty controlling anger. Todd is more impulsive and hyperactive at school than at home, but behavior at home is a problem as well.

Discussion: . . . WISC-R subtests show *considerable internal scatter.* . . .

Todd's attention deficit has been established by the Owens Rating Scale given by Dr. Hollister. The learning question is whether he is not learning in his classroom because of attentional difficulties or because of a separate learning disability.

It is my contention that the differences among Todd's WISC-R subtest scores are more the product of his attentional problems than of the kind of material presented. There is not direct evidence of learning disabilities. If Todd seems much brighter to Dr. Hollister than the IQ score she obtained, people with high Comprehension scores often seem much brighter than their Full Scale IQ because in conversation, we judge others by their comprehension. Todd's one statistically significantly weak subtest — which is not associated with any particular learning disability — would be meaningless, even without his attentional difficulty, as demonstrated below.

Lois Murphy (1973, p. 344, cited in Sattler, 1988, p. 85) writes that tests only help understand children when viewed "in relation to the child's experience in the test situation." I have reconstructed the difference between a response that would earn Todd's significantly low Similarities scaled score of 6, and a response needed for a scaled score of 9, Todd's average Verbal scaled score, as follows: For a scaled score of 6 on Similarities, a child Todd's age would earn 3 raw score points; for a scaled score of 9, 6 raw score points. To earn 3 points, he might answer the first three 1-point items; to earn 6 points, he might also answer one more 1-point item, and perhaps the first 2-point item. The difference between an average score and a significantly low one at this age is two items. For a little boy with shifting attention, this is a slender peg on which to hang a deficiency.

The attentional problems that invalidate the WISC-R findings would similarly invalidate any additional tests; therefore, it would be useless to test further. The fact that he is learning without particular difficulty in the resource room under a behavior management plan suggests that the difficulty is attention and not a learning disability.

It was recommended that behavior management be extended to his regular classroom, and further diagnostic efforts wait until Todd could maintain better attentional focus. Dr. Hollister's examination could serve to bless, rather than guide, coding decisions made on the basis of more reliable information — like Todd's response to Mariana's services. Tests are not always valid, but Todd *was* tested.

POVERTY WITHOUT ETHNICITY: TINA

Name: Tina
Age: 14-1
Grade: 7

Reason for Referral: Re-evaluation required every 3 years for continued eligibility for special services.

Background Information (source: Tina):

Early developmental information is not available. Tina says she missed a lot of kindergarten due to asthma attacks.

Tina is the eldest of five girls who live with their employed mother. The youngest is in kindergarten. When Tina was about 10, in grade 3, her father left the family, and her older brother, then 14, went with him. The following year, the family was considering a reconciliation, when her father was killed in an accident. Her brother did not return permanently to the family.

Tina is a cheerleader, enjoys informal socializing with peers, sews at home, and earns money baby-sitting.

School History:

Tina's early school records are incomplete. She helped fill in some of the missing information.

Tina attended kindergarten and grade 1, repeating kindergarten, in Kezar Falls, ME. She attended grades 2 and 3 at two different schools in Waterbury, VT. In grade 3 she had an Individual Educational Plan for 20 hours a week in a learning disabilities class. She said she did not like school until she was placed in special education, and she has liked it better since then.

The family moved to New Hampshire in grade 4. She attended school briefly in Pittsfield; then enrolled in school in Concord, where they noted her excellent behavior and effort, and did not think she needed the services projected in Vermont. By spring they had changed their minds, and wrote an IEP for the following year.

In grade 5, she transferred to this district, where she was coded learning disabled, and spent 7.5 hours a week in the resource room. Her records note lack of effort and poor marks.

In junior high, she spends the standard 3.75 hours a week in the [learning disabilities] resource room. Last year she received some warnings of failing grades.

(continued)

Tina *(continued)*

Previous Tests:

Age 11-1, The Detroit Tests of Learning Aptitude found a 9-10 age level, and low scores in auditory memory for sentences and directions.

Age 11-4, a WISC-R showed scores of VSIQ 84, PSIQ 90, FSIQ 85, with significantly low scores in auditory recall and abstract hand–eye skills.

Test Results:

Wechsler Intelligence Scale for Children — Revised
(IQ scores 90–109 and scaled scores 8–11 are in the average range. S shows a subtest significantly high for its subscale.)

Verbal Tests		Performance Tests		
Information	7	Picture Completion	5	
Similarities	7	Picture Arrangement	6	
Arithmetic	4	Block Design	8	
Vocabulary	6	Object Assembly	5	
Comprehension	6	Coding	10	S
(Digit Span)	(5)			

Verbal Scale IQ   75   Performance Scale IQ 78

Full Scale IQ   75
Mean Test Age   9-7
Grade Expectancy   4.6

Achievements:

	Grade Equivalent	Percentile Rank	Standard Score
Reading:			
Decoding: WRAT-R, Level 2	3 Beginning	1	67

Comprehension: New Sucher-Allred Reading Placement Inventory
    Independent Level: Grade 5
    Instructional Level: Grade 6
    Frustration Level: Grade 7

Written Expression:

	Grade Equivalent	Percentile Rank	Standard Score
Spelling: WRAT-R, Level 2	3 End	4	73

Writing Sample, criterion-referenced, using standards from the
    local curriculum

(continued)

Tina *(continued)*

Capitalization: appropriate
Punctuation: Grade 4
  Period in sentence (2nd +)
  Comma before quotation (4th +)
  Beginning quotation marks, but not ending (4th)
Expression: Grade 5
  Writes complete sentences (2nd +)
  Uses descriptive words (3rd +)
  Uses variety of sentences (5th +)
  Has difficulty writing complex sentences correctly (5th)
Fluency: high, produces with ease
Handwriting: teen-age pretty backhand with circular dots

Math: Criterion-referenced, using examples from the Brigance
  Inventory of Basic Skills, and standards from the local
  curriculum: Grade 5
  General knowledge of multiplication facts (3rd +)
  Multidigit multiplication: Knows process, but fast and
    inaccurate; skipped a digit she "didn't see" (5th)
  Long Divison: Does not understand some concepts needed:
    If remainder > trial divisor, try a larger divisor; Estimation
  Divides by 2 digits without 0 in quotient (4th)
  Fractions: 6th
    Addition, subtraction, multiplication of mixed fractions

Discussion:

Tina is a tall, pretty, poised, mature girl who looks about 18. She is natural, and well-oriented to the real-life world, for example, giving a school history that includes her subjective experience. She communicates well nonverbally, but her language is not adequate for discussing academic content.

The only statistically significant WISC-R subtest difference is strength in pencil skills. However, her behavior supports a nonsignificant tendency in the scores suggesting continuing auditory difficulties, which have generalized to *meaning,* even of pictures — Tina is better at non-meaningful hand–eye tasks. Verbal responses showed paucity of language and difficulty with higher-order abstractions. She maintained an objective attitude toward her work on performance tasks and knew when she was wrong, but was unable to correct her work.

(continued)

Tina *(continued)*

Despite below-grade level academic skills, her attitude was one of can-do independence. She cannot decode long multisyllabic words; she does not use such words, or know what they mean. She reads slowly. Yet she said she enjoys reading teen-age fiction and newspaper crime stories. She keeps a diary.

Summary: Tina is a slow learner whose receptive and expressive language skills are low; and the lack of development of these skills has affected (a) understanding of meaning in general, including picture material, and (b) higher-order cognition. She does best at hand–eye skills, including use of pencil, where meaning is not involved.

Tina is not underachieving. On the contrary, her rapidity on well-practiced associations and ease in pencil work bring some of her achievements above the expectancy based on the WISC-R. The WISC-R reflects largely the higher-order cognition that has suffered from her language deficits.

Tina's history is a notable beginning to a life of school difficulty. In early childhood she suffered a chronic illness which is not only exhausting but anxiety provoking, and also limits opportunities for exploratory experiences. It severely curtailed her early education.

The eldest girl in a family of seven might be expected to be delegated many housekeeping and child-rearing burdens, which might cut into study time, especially after her father left the family and mother assumed additional responsibilities. The separation from father and brother, and the death of father in place of the hoped-for reunion, raise the possibility of a family chronically depressed in response to loss.

Nevertheless, at this time, this teen-ager is a doer. She has school, domestic, social, and economic activities.

Furthermore, she is reality oriented and takes responsibility for her life. She was able to supplement the spotty school records of a child who had moved too often and supplied not only factual information, but her past emotional responses to her education as well.

The excessive absences during kindergarten caused by asthma may have been a factor in her retention. By third grade she had attended three different schools. *She did not like school until she was placed in special education, and she has liked it better since then.* By fifth grade, she had attended six different schools. (I am happy to report that the family has remained in this district ever since.) In her previous school, she was discharged from her special program, apparently because of her social skills, but within a year the learning problem again poked its horns through the curls. She must have made progress in her present program, because her hours in the resource room have been decreased. Her effort is no longer seen as consistently good, perhaps in response to the more complex assignments and increased demand for higher-order cognition of advancing grade levels.

The test on the basis of which she was first placed in a learning disabilities room is not available, so there is no way of knowing whether she ever scored in the average range. Her previous examination found her low average. Both tests given at that time converge in showing weakness in listening skills. The weakness in *abstract hand–eye skills* cited usually refers to Block Design.

Her present global and subscale scores have all slipped below low average, into the range Wechsler called "borderline," following an old practice. It once meant borderline retardation. It is not necessary to give an adaptive behavior scale to prove that Tina is not retarded. The evidence is her orientation (*well-oriented to the real-life word, helped fill in some of the missing information*), activities (*cheerleader . . . sews at home . . . earns money baby-sitting, enjoys reading teen-age fiction and newspaper crime stories, keeps a diary*), and reading comprehension (*instruction level, grade 6*). The current term is *slow learner.*

Her significant strength in Coding is consistent with a number of behaviors, *sews at home,* [written expression] *fluency high, produces with ease,* and *teen-age pretty backhand handwriting with circular dots.*

The discussion section of the report describes the language difficulties that often accompany poverty and cultural deprivation but only suggests how language difficulties in the young child often develop into difficulties in higher-order cognition, or thinking. Children who lack language concepts often fail to develop abilities in generalization, abstraction, and inference which are built on language concepts, with the result that they have difficulty thinking and reasoning about anything that is not of direct practical or emotional importance. Thinking difficulty often leads to intellectual passivity. *Records note lack of effort,* and *she . . . knew that she was wrong, but was unable to correct her work.*

Cultural deprivation is not a phrase to use in front of those it describes. Tina is white, and comes from a group whose roots go back to colonial days. They occupy the same social position as the ethnic poor. They are victims of the same forces that make ethnic people poor: Their families were in the wrong place — although they did not see it that way — at the wrong time in history; and it is difficult to improve one's economic position in the face of regional blight, family misfortune, and personal handicaps.

Tina's personal strengths and functional academic skills should help her make her way. Thinking and problem-solving skills (Feuerstein, Rand, Hoffman, & Miller, 1980) are not an intrinsic part of the remedial focus of special education, but people like Tina need them just as much to participate in an increasingly complex society.

CULTURAL DIFFERENCE WITHOUT CULTURAL TEST NORMS: BROOK

Name: Brook
Age: 7-6
Grade: 1

Reason for Referral: When the referral was first made, she was having difficulty in reading and spelling. By April she had made gains, but takes a long time to grasp concepts. Math is satisfactory.

Background Information (source: Brook and her family):

Early Development: There were no problems during pregnancy, birth, or early childhood. Brook developed earlier than her brothers and sisters, and her parents feel she is the most mature for her age of the children.

Family, Cultural: The family are full-blooded Micmac Indians and moved here from the reserve in New Brunswick, Canada, when Brook was 3.

Household members include both parents, an uncle; two sisters, 13 and 15; a brother, 12; and a male cousin, 8. An adult sister lives independently. Father and uncle are employed, and mother takes care of the family.

Interests, Activities: Brook enjoys playing a variety of active sports.

School History: Brook enrolled in kindergarten at this school at age 5-10.

A telephone call to her father brought the information that Brook has not enjoyed school this year, and her family fears she will be stigmatized by the examination.

(continued)

Brook *(continued)*

Test Results:

Kaufman Assessment Battery for Children
(IQ scores 90–109 and scaled scores 8–11 are in the average range. Scaled scores of 14 are well above average. The Band of Error shows a 90% level of confidence.)

Sequential Tests		Simultaneous Tests	
Hand Movements	9	Gestalt Closure	14
Number Recall	9	Triangles	9
Word Order	8	Matrix Analogies	10
		Spatial Memory	11
		Photo Series	10

Sequential Processing	91 ± 11	Simultaneous Processing	104 ± 11

Mental Processing Composite 100 ± 9

Simultaneous Processing > Sequential Processing at .05 confidence level

Verbal Reasoning Area from the Stanford-Binet Intelligence Scale: 4th edition (Scores 89–110 are in the average range, 79–88 in the low average range.)

Vocabulary	88
Comprehension	94
Verbal Reasoning Area	90

Achievements:

Reading:

	Grade Equivalent	Percentile Rank	Standard Score
Decoding: WRAT-R, Level 1	1 Middle	2	70

Comprehension: Does not answer reading comprehension questions on level of available reading inventory

Written Expression:

Spelling: WRAT-R, Level 1	1 End	9	80

(On local spelling series, this would be about mid-grade 1)

Writing sample, criterion-referenced, using local curriculum standards: End grade 1

(continued)

Brook *(continued)*

Capitalization: First word, name (1st)
Punctuation: Period after sentence (1st)
Sentence: Wrote a meaningful 6-word sentence (1st)

Math: End grade 1
Counts to 100. Omitted some -9s on higher numbers
Names numbers to 100
Counts objects one-to-one
Counts by 2s
Knows most number combinations to 10 automatically
Knows that if she doesn't remember, "count in your mind"

Discussion:

Brook is an attractive child of appropriate developmental status, who was becomingly dressed and wore her hair in a single braid to below her waist. She was quiet and did not offer spontaneous comments; but when asked questions about matters of importance to her, she was communicative and assertive, and knows her own mind.

The K-ABC was chosen as a test of ability because it tests learning modes rather than acquired knowledge and is therefore less influenced by cultural factors than the more conventional IQ tests. In addition, there are three possible teaching or modeling items on each subtest. Brook learns very well by having someone model a task for her. Her Simultaneous Processing (all visual) is significantly higher than her Sequential Processing, but both are in the average range. There are no statistically significant differences among subtests.

Because the K-ABC does not test verbal skills, the Verbal Reasoning Area of the Stanford-Binet IV, a more conventional IQ test, was also given to supplement the K-ABC. Brook's Verbal Reasoning is also average.

Brook takes a logical approach to tasks and carries through each whole task. She particularly enjoyed a subtest where each item began with the same stylized question; and when I felt it was no longer necessary to repeat it, she took to repeating the question herself for each new item.

Brook is very sensitive to failure and, although she did not explain what was bothering her, she seemed hurt by challenging items necessary for establishing a ceiling.

(continued)

Brook *(continued)*

Summary: Brook has normal ability. She is grade-appropriate in written expression and math, and has gotten a foothold in reading decoding, but is not yet able to decode and comprehend at the same time. She does not have any learning disabilities. Her hand–eye skills are probably better than her auditory-language skills. She is the kind of child served by Chapter I and Remedial Reading.

Although she does not have learning disabilities, she has a definite learning style. She likes a calm, quiet atmosphere. She does not like to be singled out for attention, particularly in front of the class. She needs modeling and explanation, followed by practice, and more modeling if necessary. She enjoys reciting repetitively and might enjoy reciting facts to be learned in unison in a group. She does not like to take risks. She needs to be taught in small steps and to have generalizations pointed out to her until she can make the leap herself. Given the learning atmosphere she needs, she will eventually feel secure enough to take a more adventurous approach.

Brook's learning style is somewhat at variance with the teaching style in many current classrooms, where the environment is busy, many things are going on at once, children are expected to be active, learning is often individual rather than group, and children are given a wide array of choices and challenged to learn independently from experience.

Recommendations: Brook is not educationally handicapped. She might receive Chapter I and Remedial Reading services if she qualifies. Selection of her future teachers might be guided by the discussion of her learning style above.

The Micmac Indians of eastern Canada and northern New England are recognized by the Canadian government and the state of Maine, which makes educational benefits available, but not by the United States, although a Maine group has applied for U.S. acknowledgment. Brook's family considers their citizenship to be in the North American Indian nation, of both the United States and Canada.

They are a proud, self-supporting, intact, extended family group that moved to the United States from the reserve in Canada in search of a better life for their children. They do not always accept the school's every decision. *Her family fears she will be stigmatized by the examination. Brook has not enjoyed school this year.* They see Brook as a special child, not in the sense of "special" education, but in a positive way. *She is the most mature for her age of the children.* They want her to have a better future than an older child who strayed from the path, *an adult sister lives independently,* and they are apprehensive about Brook's experiences.

Why has she not enjoyed school? One hypothesis is that she was slow to catch on to decoding and encoding, and the difficulty was frustrating to her. In view of her adequate achievements by the end of the year, the possibility of a different reason should remain a silent question in the examination.

The K-ABC proved an excellent choice for Brook. The test results bear out its cultural fairness. Furthermore, it provided the opportunity for her best way of learning, from modeling and explanation. I decided not to treat the significant difference between Sequential and Simultaneous scales as the answer to the referral question because they are both in the average range—no sequential deficit—and because the learning preferences she displayed were not related to a simultaneous learning style. Simultaneous learners tend to be field-independent. Brook is a very conservative learner. She wants quiet, structure, routine, and someone to lead her in small steps.

Brook's teacher had a teaching style that works well with young children from many cultural groups: She had a vivacious, enthusiastic personality, was able to coordinate many different simultaneous individual activities, and stimulated pupil participation by her high activity level and vocal encouragement. This was exactly the opposite of Brook's needs, and she withdrew. As a result of the examination, a quiet teacher with a quiet, single-focus classroom was chosen for Brook for the next year.

More recently, to learn more of the cultural perspective, I called the nearest native American organization, the Abenaki, closely related to the Micmacs. The spokesperson[2] there said that in her experience, many native American girls have the same learning characteristics described in Brook's report. She emphasized the need for a quiet learning environment and dislike of taking risks.

6 THE SOCIAL, ORGANIZATIONAL, AND POLITICAL CONTEXT OF CLINICAL INFERENCE

Most school examiners do not see themselves in a historical light, but as toilers in an educational back 40 acres, performing concrete practical tasks that serve the broader purpose of helping children get an education. But drawing inferences, like any other activity, is done in a sociological and historical setting that shapes its course and results (Mannheim, 1936/1968). Conclusions about the children are a result of certain times and organizations and are influenced by social trends and organizational relationships.

Social, *organizational,* and *political* influences are somewhat arbitrary and overlapping. *Social* refers to influences that are a product of the times we live in. *Organizational* refers to the influence of the organizations where most people confront the larger society. One way organizations exert influence is through their regulations. The term *political* is used here in a more restricted sense than the popular use: It refers only to internal politics — power relations among individuals. It does not refer to political parties, or community politics like school budget disputes and interethnic strife. These issues usually influence school examiners through organizational channels.

One of the best known examples of community issues affecting examiners through organizational policies is the long and hotly contested 1971 *Larry P.* decision in the U.S. Court of Appeals for the Ninth Circuit, that IQ tests no longer be used to classify minority group children for special education (Lambert, 1981; "Perspectives," 1987).

This case affects examiners primarily through organizational policies and regulations mandating their testing practices. The effects of *Larry P.* would fall within the present use of the term *political* only when differences of opinion about the case affect relationships at work.

The term *political* has been reserved for personal politics in hope that this influence will not be overlooked as too petty for serious attention.

THE SOCIAL CONTEXT

The changes in society since the beginning of the testing movement in the 19-teens and 20s, have changed not only successive generations of tests, but the way society uses them.

1. **Scientific and technological changes,** foremost among them *quantification* and *computerization,* have changed psychology and education. The historical and continuing importance of quantification in psychology is discussed in the Introduction (pp. xi-xii). It has influenced education through their mutual branch, educational psychology.

The effect of quantification on clinical inference has been that numerical information tends to be more highly regarded than descriptive information, and statistical reasoning more highly regarded than logical reasoning. These values promote the mechanical level of test interpretation in preference to the individualized level.

Computerization has eased routine clerical burdens for school districts and is considered the key to the future for a generation of students on their way to the job market. It is only a step to considering *all* computerized processes better than their alternatives. Add the pressure on staff to turn out ever more work, and the result is computerization of procedures that were better individualized.

Computerization requires ready-made categories for reporting data. Ready-made categories (see Chapter 2, p. 23) do not provide for the variety and range of behavior illustrated in Chapter 2. Even where *None of the Above* or *Other* is a choice, it is a blind-end choice that does not lead to any conclusions, for no conclusions from *Other* can be known in advance to be programmed. The result is to discourage examiners from conceptualizing categories suggested by the data and to frustrate those who do.

Computerization also yields ready-made conclusions. Computerized conclusions are derived from scores alone. When behavior is entered in the computer in the ready-made categories, the information appears in the report as window-dressing only, without entering into the conclusions. The result is the mechanical level of interpretation.

The implied superiority of computers means that where computerized conclusions are available, *even though only intended as hypotheses,* they tend to become the standard against which clinical inference is judged. The result is to make mechanical interpretation seem superior to individualized interpretation.

2. **Bureaucracy** is not only a modern problem. It also characterized administration in past complex societies—large, old, and fragmented societies. Bureaucracy represents control that is not only external, but distant and unresponsive, taking little account of local and individual circumstances.

School districts of all sizes feel the impact of bureaucracy in the administration of the Individuals with Disabilities Education Act (IDEA), of being controlled from afar and burdened with petty stipulations and paperwork. The contact point is the agencies and departments that make up the organizational context, discussed on pp. 178-181.

Bureaucracy produces feelings of frustration and helplessness among the governed. It leads to fatalism, phrased as the impossibility of fighting city hall, the superintendent's office, the state department of education, etc. Under bureaucracy, because examiners do not *own* their work, they become alienated and are likely not to try to do the best possible job, but just the minimum necessary. Because bureaucracy represents and promotes fragmentation, examiners are less likely to reach for a holistic explanation that covers all the data.

3. **A centralization of power** is taking place in organizations that employ most of the middle class, with accompanying increased overt domination and confrontation: The iron hand has taken off the velvet glove. A generation ago middle-class people saw large organizations as their opportunity and benefactor. Now there is a sense that the social contract between organizations and employees has been broken. Disillusionment has reached the point that small individual enterprise is seen as preferable to employment. Those who remain with organizations know they must either confront every infringement or put up with the consequences.

This centralization provides opportunities for individuals who are personally hungry for power to rise by serving organizational goals. In the growing bureaucracy serving the Individuals with Disabilities Education Act (IDEA), supervisors may be appointed who have very superficial knowledge of some of the areas under their supervision. Examiners face an increased likelihood that their administrators will impose inappropriate controls on examinations. Specific examples are discussed under political influences (pp. 181-184).

4. Associated with centralization of power in organizations is the **extension of the principle of division of labor to middle-class employees,** with resulting feelings of alienation the same as those of their blue-collar counterparts in the same situation. Examiners find that under these conditions, the self-actualization (Maslow, 1954/1987) motives that originally called them to their work are no longer tenable, and they lose their sense of professional purpose. School psychologists in particular do not see it as their role to be told to "give a quick IQ test for coding," as certificate-holders rather than as participants in educational problem solving. The result is general alienation and disillusionment with testing. Some spokespersons for the school psychology profession (see Whelan & Carlson, 1986) have proposed leaving testing to others whose self-concept is less incompatible with the assembly-line worker's role.

5. **Social factionalization and contentiousness** are on the increase. They are related to a positive change — greater self-awareness and hope among parts of the population once resigned to a lesser share in the society. Since this change began among ethnic minorities, many other groups have tried to share their moral power by considering themselves minority groups too — and intensified the social splintering. Television role-models have turned confrontation into acceptable everyday manners.

Parents view school as another oppressor. Contentiousness is seen as appropriate behavior in the middle-class workplace. The effect on clinical inference has been the expectation of conflict over test results, and consequent retreat from creative clinical inference to the "safer" kind with universal-access results: convergent thinking, mechanical-level interpretation, and achievement tests with elaborate statistical norms but little opportunity to observe academic skill behavior. Such achievement tests serve the purpose of proof better than discovery. (See Chapter 4, pp. 79-80.) Chapters 1 and 3 have shown the discovery model to be superior to the proof model for diagnosis. This is especially true for initial diagnosis in the early grades, when there is less opportunity for supporting information from school records; and the beginning grades curriculum is too close to the bottom of the test range, and varies too much among schools, to depend on scores like *Grade Equivalent 1.2.*

6. Related to contentiousness is increased **litigiousness:** the tendency to use lawsuits to settle matters that would once have been resolved less formally, less angrily, and less expensively. The effects on clinical inference have been an intensification of the effects of contentiousness,

discussed above. Because inferences may be checked against another examiner and ultimately decided on by a judge who is untrained in the field, proof becomes much more important than discovery. The desirable examination, then, is the safe, convergent, mechanical, lowest common denominator that produces no striking insights. The threat of litigation is a strong argument in favor of an inferior kind of clinical inference.

7. **The Individuals with Disabilities Education Act (IDEA)** has become a social force in itself, and its provisions and definitions have influenced clinical inference.

Team participation.   A result of the team participation provision is the concept of *truth as consensus.* The right answer is neither the one that corresponds to the real situations (correspondence truth) nor the one that makes sense (coherence truth); but unanimous or majority opinion (consensus truth), modeled after the jury system and the electoral process rather than scientific investigation. The consensus concept of truth has changed the political relationship of examiner to consultee (see pp. 181-184). It becomes another force toward convergent, mechanical interpretation, with examiners trying to predict team opinion instead of leading it.

Team participation is founded on equality of interest, not equality of knowledge. Specialists are team members because of professional expertise in their area. Mechanical interpretation, wrongly used as equalizer and standardizer, drives out talented examiner-interpreters and leaves the field to technicians.

Intelligence testing as part of the evaluation process.   There is a concept of intelligence that has grown out of the need to evaluate intelligence and learning disabilities simultaneously for the identification of learning disabilities under IDEA. It is *the ability to manipulate ("process") a great deal of information, and do it fast.* This concept values speed and facility over power and depth. The tests are not to blame. They have been developed in response to public need. The manipulation of information has always been present to some degree in intelligence tests. Wechsler increased its proportion of the test, and it occupies an even greater proportion of current tests like the Kaufman Assessment Battery for Children and the Stanford-Binet: 4th edition. The K-ABC is *all* processing. Speed has a more prominent role in Wechsler's than in other tests. In his test for school ages, it is a major factor distinguishing among age-norms for hand–eye skills at the higher age-levels. Process takes precedence over product, and achievement is less important than how soon it happens.

This concept of intelligence is far from Alfred Binet's (Binet & Simon, 1916/1980, pp. 42-43) choice of *judgment* as the essential activity of intelligence. Binet's definition fitted a society changing slowly enough to evaluate answers. The *processing* definition fits a society where there are no answers, because answers obsolesce, like practitioners' rules; and a smart person is not one who can figure out the answers, but who can do new things fast.

The processing concept of intelligence may predict learning in children in the skill acquisition stage of development, but examiners easily extend the definition to themselves. Applied to adults, it devalues taking time to put things together and think them through and therefore encourages the instant solutions of mechanical associations at the expense of incubation and creative problem solving.

Another assumption associated with intelligence testing is that *there is more or less one right answer, and it is in the manual.* From there, it is easy to see referral questions as having one convergent answer that is approximately the same for all respondents. But it is possible for a question to have more than one right answer, and there are many questions for which the best answer is yet to be found.

THE ORGANIZATIONAL CONTEXT

More frustrations with work are caused by its organizational context than by the work itself. The organizational context includes the regulations and expectations of school systems and state departments of education.

The foremost regulation for school examiners is the Individuals with Disabilities Education Act (IDEA), the 1990 revision of the 1975 Education for All Handicapped Act. Those who think IDEA is bad are too young to remember school before any help was available except an isolated and stigmatized self-contained room for the supposedly mentally retarded, which often included students with IQs up to 100 who were behavior problems or could not get academic help any other way.

Once, however, children are taken out of their classrooms for special help, even for one period, the invisible dunce cap that is part of Western tradition is immediately passed on to the next lowest child, who would have been considered unremarkable had the three formerly lowest not been coded. The teacher then worries about this child, who is having difficulty with an increasingly difficult elementary curriculum (Elkind, 1988)—and refers for testing.

There are now usually two administrative hierarchies in schools: the regular administrative structure, and special education. Examiners who work under regular administrators come under pressure to get the discipline problems out of the regular classroom and into special education. Examiners under special education fare better in this respect but, if they are school psychologists, are unhappy at lack of opportunities to serve the nonhandicapped population and use consultation skills to support the teaching staff.

Organizational Constraints on Examiners

Whichever hierarchy they are under, there are almost certain to be organizational constraints upon examiners.

Production: Making the Rate

School systems, with limited budgets and unlimited referrals for testing, need as many examinations as possible for the money. One widespread production standard is that examiners should test three children a week. Far-ranging similarity is usually not a coincidence, but points to a common source. I have not been able to locate this source, but national associations are often the springs of homogeneous standards.

As an independent contractor, working at my own pace, on my own time, it is easy for me to give three or more examinations a week. When I was an employee, however, it was not possible, because (1) many additional duties were assigned that did not count toward production figures; (2) working conditions were often detrimental to efficiency, especially in report writing; and (3) during some periods, internal politics claimed an inordinate share of productive energy. The resulting conflict between career and emotional survival, on one hand, and motivation to do a good examination, on the other, can dilute the quality of examinations.

Defining Handicapping Conditions: Learning Disabilities

The definition of a learning disability has not yet been settled for all time.[1] Teams are usually more concerned with the more practical matter of the evaluation criterion, a "severe discrepancy between achievement and intellectual ability." This criterion leaves room for considerable flexibility; it also allows more precise redefinition.

Many states and districts have defined *severe discrepancy* for their own use, at least in part to prevent an ever-increasing number of children from being identified as learning disabled. Limiting expenditures, however, is not the only purpose. Control — setting standards and making regulations — is a basic activity of public organizations.

From some sources at hand: The Ohio State Department of Education (Telzrow & Williams, 1982) defines a severe discrepancy as 2.00 standard deviations or more between a test of ability and a test of achievement. The second draft of revised criteria by the Minnesota Department of Education (1990) uses 1.88 standard deviations or more. The Lansing, Michigan, School District (1989) uses 1.5 standard deviations or more. Some of these materials offer more specific information for comparing particular tests, based on a regression formula using the intertest correlations. New Hampshire, the state whose motto is "Live free or die," on the other hand, has appropriately not mandated a precise numerical discrepancy. In fact, New Hampshire has published, although not officially endorsed, a guide that decries this practice (Willis, 1990).

Some districts add another requirement for identification as a learning-disabled student: an IQ test score of 90 or above.

Such precise numerical criteria have the following effects on clinical inference:

1. Examiners are not free to choose the most appropriate testing instrument.

Numerical criteria are almost always expressed in standard deviations, which require standard scores for comparison. This leads to regulations that only *tests with standard scores* be given, and sometimes leads to a state-approved test list.

Achievement tests with standard scores often, in the interest of objective scoring, *omit the kind of material that provides an opportunity for the examiner to gain insight into the subject's skills* in that area. This is especially true in reading comprehension. The reading inventories that reading specialists prefer, standardized in whole-grade intervals, are numerically crude in comparison; but they provide rich opportunities for observation of reading behavior.

Achievement tests with standard scores are also often *contaminated* with factors irrelevant to the skill tested. In reading comprehension, the irrelevant factor on one test is comprehension of a set of complicated pictures that must be compared while remembering a sentence previously read. On another test it is grammatic closure. Bilingual and language-disabled students often cannot correctly fill in blanks in the middle of sentences even though they understand intact reading matter of equivalent difficulty. In math computation, absent-minded people are penalized for ignoring operations signs.

Achievement tests with standard scores have *national norms*, which are not appropriate in some regions. Northern New England, where I work now, has high achievement norms. A student can have an average score on national norms and be far behind in the local curriculum.

The result of having to use less appropriate tests is decreased quality motivation and alienation from work.

2. Precise numerical definitions express administrative categories rather than educational and psychological ones. Examiners who are preoccupied with administrative and bureaucratic aspects of testing become distracted from professional aspects. They should be seeking causes of behavior, not applying formulas.

3. Precise numerical definitions lead to intellectual dishonesty and cynicism, as examiners juggle tests and subtests in an effort to obtain scores needed. Testing is used, not to learn about the child, but to justify decisions reached independently.

4. Requiring nationally standardized achievement tests is out of keeping with the goals of the school psychology profession, which favors locally and more simply defined curriculum-based assessment (National Association of School Psychologists, 1986). External standards imposed on professional activities contribute to the disillusionment of the profession with the testing role.

THE POLITICAL CONTEXT

The influences considered here are those resulting from power relations among individuals. They are ad hoc decisions by persons in power, rather than formal organizational policies. Sometimes they are a deliberate attempt to take away the power of the examiner to draw inferences and reach conclusions independent of the administrator's. More often they are made in the interest of efficiency or practicality, like using a collection of partial test findings by the staff on hand, instead of the integrated conclusions of an outside examiner.

Constraints Resulting from Power Relations

Casting the Examiner in the Pair-of-Hands Role

Specifying tests. As has been stated in another context (pp. 179-181), when examiners are not free to choose the instruments that seem to them most appropriate, they are less able to seek the information they need for a holistic synthesis.

Specifying categories for collecting data or giving conclusions. Ready-made categories, as discussed in Chapter 2, p. 23, may miss the most important point. They promote convergent thinking by leading the examiner away from independent conceptualization.

Ordering test results. It may seem incongruous to some, but examiners are sometimes told what results to find.

I was once dispatched to a distant district to test a child in foster care. Her mother lived in our district, and state regulations held the district of the mother's residence responsible for the tuition of children receiving any special education services. I was instructed to obtain an IQ between 80 and 89 so she would not be eligible for any special education code. I failed this assignment. The child seemed dull in the initial interview. I chose the Kaufman Assessment Battery for Children in hope of getting beyond some of her cultural deprivation. To my chagrin, the K-ABC compensated more than expected, and she scored 92. I was met by my administrator's wrath, followed by a memo prohibiting the use of the K-ABC in the district, and the disappearance of the two K-ABC kits from the supply closet.

The test as mere ritual. "Just give an IQ test and let us interpret it," is a demand for concrete-level interpretation. The political implication is that the examiner does not have the stature and regard of others to draw conclusions. "Give an IQ test so we can code LD — we've already done everything else" downgrades testing to a clerical routine, and the examiner to a paraprofessional.

The Administrator as Clinical Supervisor

Draw me a map. The requirement that all inferences be supported in the report implies that the administrator has to approve their validity. It places the administrator in the role of the examiner's *clinical* supervisor. The examiner should be able to support conclusions when asked, with answers geared to particular questions and persons asking; but complete paper documentation is not necessary for qualified staff.

Misconception of the Multidisciplinary Approach

Team participation means members of different disciplines review the case together, as consultants if they have not had direct contact. It does not mean that a member of each discipline has to give the child a whole or partial test battery. Yet it is sometimes interpreted this way, and this interpretation has political consequences:

Assembly-line testing. This method might be called, in contemporary terms, The Six Visually Impaired Persons and the Elephant. Unless the team is a close-knit working unit, division of labor deters holistic interpretation and keeps it fragmented and concrete or mechanical. It also takes away the examiner's power to integrate data toward conclusions and gives this power to the administrator.

Overtesting. Misconception of the multidisciplinary approach can lead to the situation discussed in Chapter 4, pp. 95-97, where increasing the number of tests given increases the likelihood of mistaking chance effects for real ones.

A concrete "peaks and valleys" concept of learning disabilities can lead to this situation: The team would like to code a certain child learning disabled. The first test does not show any significant weaknesses. They ask another specialist to give another test. Eventually a significantly weak subtest turns up. The team is pleased; this is the learning disability they were looking for. Sometimes a contest atmosphere develops, where the person who gives the test that obtains a significant weakness is judged best examiner.

There would be less occasion for overtesting if teams' concept of learning disabilities were based on the learning process instead of the test pattern.

The Place of the Examiner in the Local Political Unit

The political atmosphere of the team is a subtle factor, and difficult to document in a professional manner; but it does exist, as team members all admit in private moments.

To do a good job of clinical inference, the examiner must be politically free to draw divergent, holistic, individualized conclusions instead of the convergent, fragmented, mechanical conclusions that everyone else on the team can draw without seeing the child. If the examiner does not have the team's support, this cannot be.

Contemporary people consider themselves more enlightened than those of the historical past, when authoritarian church and state were the agencies in the struggle for power in the society. That struggle is not dead. We feel superior to the age when Galileo, under threat of death, muttered under his breath, as he publicly denied that the earth moves around the sun, "But it *does* move." In our society people are not executed for voicing the wrong scientific opinion. The penalty is humiliation, job change or loss of employment, and sometimes ostracism and career change.[2] It can still be very difficult to stand up for one's conclusions. Some examiners have muttered, after a public statement to the contrary, "But he *is* educationally handicapped."

7 CONCLUSIONS

Tests used in learning evaluations yield scores that are used to obtain diagnostic information. The diagnostic information is sought at least as eagerly as the scores.

Diagnostic use of learning tests is often mistakenly restricted to interpretation of the profile of test scatter, whether the tests were designed to yield diagnostic profiles, like the Kaufman Assessment Battery for Children and the Stanford-Binet Intelligence Scale: 4th edition; or whether the diagnostic indicators were discovered afterwards, as on the Wechsler scales.

Profile interpretation has two bases. One is *empirical research*. This is the basis for interpretations of the Wechsler Verbal–Performance discrepancy, and factors like the three-factor system, Verbal Comprehension, Perceptual Organization, and Freedom from Distractibility. These empirically based, statistically derived generalizations are the basis for the *mechanical level of interpretation* described in Chapter 1, pp. 8-11. The application of statistical generalizations to the individual contains a riddle: Do these odds fit this person or not?

The other basis for profile interpretation is *content analysis*. This is the basis for subtest interpretation. Generalizations about subtest content are the basis for the *concrete level of interpretation* described in Chapter 1, pp. 1-7. Because any subtest is influenced by a number of different factors, the application of content analysis to individuals involves the same riddle as statistical generalizations: Does the generalization fit this person?

Figure 9. Psychology has two faces, one turned toward the population and one toward the individual.

The science of psychology has two faces, one turned toward the population and one toward the individual (Figure 9). Research psychologists are concerned primarily with the population, and practitioners with the individual. This difference in orientation leads to misunderstandings.

Test scores are the application of complex statistical generalizations — the means and standard deviations of population samples, on variables selected to represent complex theoretical concepts — to individuals who are presumably from the same population on which the generalizations were developed. These generalizations are free of nonessential details; their application tells what they were designed to tell, and it does not tell anything else. They have the flaw of all generalizations. The details passed-by in their design as nonessential may, in individual cases, be important information for answering the question the tests are designed, or used, to answer. Their measurements are precise, but they have the same potential for misuse as all measurements. They measure very well, but they do not always measure the same thing, and they do not tell what they are measuring.

Tests provide another kind of information in addition to the scores they were designed to give. Test items are small samples of presumably characteristic behavior in a standardized situation. They are like pinholes through which to view larger daily functioning. In administering tests, examiners observe samples of many individuals' behavior. As they become familiar with tests, they internalize informal behavior norms. These norms enable them to recognize behavior that follows familiar patterns (prototypes), and behavior that calls for fresh problem solving.

Chapter 3 showed that behavior and other information sometimes support scores and sometimes contradict them. The reason there is sometimes contradiction is the difference between the way scores are derived—statistically, from the population—and the way they are applied—specifically, to the individual. In case of contradiction, the practitioner must determine for each case whether the conclusions follow the scores, or the behavior, or other information.

Individuals' test scores are the product of many factors that influence the scores as vectors. The action of these influences, which can often be observed directly in test behavior, sometimes distorts the scores. Scores are like shadows on a wall. This analogy comes from Plato's (ca. 385 B.C./1892, pp. 253-257) Allegory of the Cave (see Figure 10 and Appendix 2), where people look at shadows instead of the objects

Figure 10.   Shadows and reality: Plato's Allegory of the Cave.

that cast them, and mistake the shadows for the real things. Shadows do not show the whole picture, but we can only measure shadows. Sometimes shadows accurately reflect the objects that cast them, and sometimes they are deceptive. (See Figure 11.) Test behavior enables examiners to look at the reality behind the shadows, and judge how accurate or how distorted the shadows are, before basing further judgments on their measurements.

There is a solution to the riddle of how to apply generalizations of uncertain fit to individuals. The solution is to check the generalizations against individual information—test behavior and background—for fit and coherence. This is the *individualized level of interpretation* introduced in Chapter 1, pp. 12-20, and illustrated throughout the book. It consists of looking at the events that produce the particular test responses to find the reasons for the scores, and inferring whether, for this person, the scores represent the same abilities as in the standardization sample or the accumulated lore, or whether the scores have some different, individual meaning that cannot be understood without looking at the events of the testing session and past history. The use of behavioral observations and background information to decide whether scores fit individual test subjects makes examinations *individually interpreted as well as individually administered*.

Individualized interpretation does not mean disregarding test scores. Test scores are the population data, and test behavior and background information are the individual data. Behavior and background must be cross-checked against scores just as scores are checked against behavior and background. *Failure to thrive* has one meaning with an IQ of 60 and another with an IQ of 95. *Perplexity* has one meaning with an IQ of 82 and another with an IQ of 112. *Ambidextrousness* has one meaning with academic underachievement and another with adequate or superior achievement.

There are two reasons why individualized test interpretation is not more widespread: (1) Teaching it is a labor-intensive, individualized process involving instructor feedback and student self-correction. Proficient people tend to be largely self-taught. (2) A number of social, organizational, and political forces have influenced testing practice in the direction of the mechanical and concrete levels of interpretation. These same influences have contributed to the disillusionment of the school psychology profession with the testing role. This has some dangers for the profession, as testing has traditionally been psychologists' special, if not exclusive, terrain; and a special terrain insures professional survival. But there are even more dangers to testing. All-in-all, no group of examiners tests as well as psychologists, or defends testing as vigorously

Figure 11.   Sometimes shadows accurately reflect the objects that cast them, and sometimes they are deceptive. Right — Illustration by H. Thiriat, from "Shadowgraphy" by H. R. Evans, 1911, in A. A. Hopkins, *Magic: Stage Illusions and Scientific Diversions,* pp. 173-183. New York: Scientific American [Munn]. (Original work published 1897)

from organizational abuse. Testing needs psychologists more than psychologists need testing.

Individualization cuts both ways. Not only is the test subject an individual; the examiner is an individual too. The examiner has the special position of being the only person to observe the test behavior. With this exclusive information, examiners should not be expected to reach the same conclusions as those team members who have only armchair knowledge.

In an earlier period of educational-psychological testing, examiners were scarce experts. Their habitat was university clinics and the central offices of the more urban or affluent school systems. Examiners were considered competent if their individual conclusions had the ring of credibility (coherence truth).

Since the increase in testing required by the Individuals with Disabilities Education Act (IDEA), examiners have become numerous and familiar. The team participation provision of IDEA has sometimes been interpreted that any member's opinion about anything is as good as any other's, or that the majority opinion is correct (consensus truth). For replaceable cogs in a special education or mental health machine, the touchstone of competence has become drawing exactly the same conclusions as most other people. A perceptive examiner may be criticized for not parroting the lowest common denominator. This situation does not encourage individualized interpretation.

Recommendations

As in test reports, conclusions lead to recommendations. For the encouragement of individualized testing—*truth from testing*—the following recommendations are offered for examiners, administrators of many levels, and the examiners' professions (see Introduction, Note 4) as a whole.

For Examiners:

1. Examiners should use descriptive and background information as well as test scores in drawing conclusions and pay particular attention to learning-related test behavior.

For Local Administrators and Examiners:

2. Efforts should be made to have a team atmosphere of mutually respecting persons working together.

3. One examiner should complete enough of an examination to have the opportunity to form a holistic conception of the person and the problem.

4. Diagnosis—the naming, or explanation of the cause of the problem—sometimes needs to be separate from identification of a handicapping condition. One does not necessarily lead to the other. The various disciplines represented on the team specialize in their own disorders and explanations, and their most relevant and helpful categories do not necessarily coincide with the codes and definitions of the Individuals with Disabilities Education Act. Examiners diagnose better when they conceptualize problems in terms of their professional training, rather than in terms of regulations classifications. Sometimes a diagnosis clearly identifies a handicapping condition, but often it does not. At these times, the team should let the examiner diagnose, and the examiner let the team code.

For Makers of State and Local Regulations, Local Administrators, and Examiners:

5. Test choice should be left to the examiner.

    a. Examiners need to be able to choose tests they are comfortable with, to help them reach holistic conclusions.

    b. Tests should satisfy professional peer review rather than administrative considerations.

    c. Tests should be chosen for diagnostic helpfulness rather than statistical elegance.

d. Local culture should be respected by allowing use of tests with standards appropriate for the locality.

6. People providing evaluative information should not be given ready-made sets of categories for reporting, which supposedly cover all the possibilities. They need open-ended choice to be free to discover new categories (see Chapter 2, p. 23) and explanations (pp. 106-109).

For the Professions (See Introduction, Note 4), **Makers of State and Local Regulations, Local Administrators, and Examiners:**

7. The problem of defining learning disabilities should be solved, not by imposing rigid numerical criteria, but by clarifying the underlying concept.

8. The term *behavioral* should replace the word "clinical" to describe individualized test interpretation, in such phrases as *behavioral signs,* and *behavioral interpretation.* The term *behavior* has high status in psychology and would improve the scientific status of clinical inference.

*   *   *

If individualized test interpretation is not encouraged, but is allowed to be driven out by the mechanical and concrete interpretation that have become popular, testing will eventually be discredited as a way to understand individuals. Its rituals will continue to be performed to satisfy regulations requirements, but those who seek to understand individuals will have to look to an avenue other than tests.

Sometimes situations have a reverse effect. I once worked in a place where the political cards were stacked so high that there was no satisfaction to be found in the team process or relationships with colleagues. It drove me into myself. I asked why I had gone into this work. The answer was to understand individual behavior directly. Although the goal was ambitious, the needs were modest: no tuition or laboratory, just a job in the field. I could work toward my goal alone, despite unfriendly fire and lack of formal learning opportunities.

I began by writing down observations of all the behavior that occurred during testing; not the bare-bones observations of *Psych 101,* but the mixed-level observations of a qualified practitioner, who sometimes interprets behavior on the spot, and sometimes suspends judgment. I tried to weave these into a unified picture of a person's behavior and functioning. That was the beginning. It was not long before these pictures were integrated with the test results and background material to answer the referral questions. They answered them very well. This book is one result.

APPENDIX 1
TESTING AS THERAPY: PAUL

Testing and therapy are generally seen as separate activities: Therapy is seen as the crowning service that actually helps people, whereas school testing is often regarded as a preliminary ritual that is the admission price to the helping services. Some even consider testing potentially harmful, in the same way danger of trauma accompanies invasive medical procedures. Establishing a test ceiling means asking children questions they cannot answer, with the possible resulting perception of failure and frustration. Yet an examination provides a rare opportunity for examiner and child to explore together the circumstances and realities of school and life. Sometimes they reach the incidental reward of shared discovery and its aftermath.

Paul illustrates the unplanned therapeutic effects that can come out of a school psychological examination.

There is a small private day school in my district with about 200 students in grades 1 through 8. These children are entitled to psychological services from the school district. They are not, however, referred for these services in anywhere near the numbers of a public school the same size, for reasons found in similar schools everywhere. The children are selected on the basis of their parents' motivation to give them an education they consider superior. These parents firmly support the authority of the school and the teachers. Public schools envy these advantages. There is also a staff ethic that can best be described as wishing to exhaust obvious, traditional measures before trying to superimpose anything as exotic as school psychology on a system that has flourished for many centuries without it. For these reasons, I am asked to come there only three or four times a year.

For 5 years I kept hearing about Paul. My profession reminded them of him. He was a serious case, whose shocking, violent history was recounted by successive consultees. But although each time they told his story I said I would be glad to see him, he was not referred. This omission was not an oversight. There is a ripening process in human affairs, a right time to intervene. They preferred tolerating his behavior to upsetting the balance. A consulting outsider must reckon with the chosen pace.

The confluence of two changes brought about a referral. One was the appointment of a no-nonsense new principal, call her Denise. The other was Paul's entry into adolescence.

<u>To</u>: Director of Special Services
    Paul's Home Town, Another State

<u>Name</u>: Paul
<u>Age</u>: 14-6
<u>Grade</u>: 8
<u>School</u>: Valley Academy, Our Town, This State
<u>Principal</u>: Denise Tatro
<u>Teacher</u>: Kenneth Johnston

<u>Reason for Referral</u>: Defiant classroom behavior: refusal to do schoolwork; verbal disrespect to teachers.

<u>Background Information</u> (Sources: previous consultation notes; interviews with Paul's teacher, principal, and great-aunt):

Paul is the youngest of eight children. In his early years, he suffered and witnessed family violence which culminated in the death of one of his parents. His great-aunt then brought him to this community to live with her. He sometimes returned to relatives in his home town, but each time she brought him back. She has always had difficulty managing him. She has indulged him to make up for the past. She is now in frail health. Now that he is a teen-ager, he demands to go out evenings and week-ends. She has so far managed to prevent this.

Mr. Johnston says Paul is polite and pleasant to teachers out of school, but defiant in school.

(continued)

Paul *(continued)*

School History: Paul entered grade 1 at Valley Academy, age 6-3, and repeated grade 1. Grades were Cs at the beginning, but by grade 3 were almost all Ds. There have been behavior problems over the years. Last year there were many absences. There was a question whether he wanted to stay home, or his [great-] aunt needed him there.

Group Test Data: Most achievement scores over the years have been below grade level. Scores have shown large fluctuations over the years. Last year's scores indicated a minimal functional level, although below grade.

Ability/Academic Test Results; Personality Tests Given:

Wechsler Intelligence Scale for Children—Revised (incomplete)

Verbal Tests		Performance Tests	
Information	6	Picture Completion	8
Similarities	7		

Achievements:

Reading:

Decoding: Wide-Range Achievement Test   Grade 7.2

Comprehension: Stanford Diagnostic Reading Test:
(administered by Mr. Johnston)   Grade 5.8

Literal Comprehension	Stanine 2
Inferential Comprehension	Stanine 4
Total Comprehension	Stanine 3

Highest reading level reached (total
success on one paragraph)   9.0

Written Expression:

Criterion-referenced writing sample, using standards from the
Test of Written English: Estimate Grade 4

Capitalization: some proper nouns   Grade 4

Punctuation: Grade 2
Uses period at end of sentence
Uses exclamation point in exclamatory sentence
Does not use question mark or comma

Sentences: Sentence structure grade-appropriate

(continued)

Paul *(continued)*

Spelling: No standardized test given   Estimate Grade 3 to 4

In the writing sample, he spelled correctly *Atlantic, practice, yelled;* and misspelled *can't, hurray, patience*

Math: Wide-Range Achievement Test (administered by Mr. Johnston)   Grade 5.0

Skills shown: Multiplies and divides by 1 digit
             Does simple fractions and percent

Personality Tests Given:

Diagnostic Interview
Drawings: Person (male, female), Tree
2 cards from the Rorschach (ink-blot) Test (remainder rejected)
Sentence Completion Test (administered by Mr. Johnston)

Discussion of Ability/Achievement Tests; Findings of Personality Tests:

Paul is a slender boy of average development, in early adolescence. He has begun to grow in height, but not yet in weight. He is well-groomed and well-dressed. His face has a prematurely tough, wise expression. His nails are bitten close.

He had a mixed response to the interview and tests. He resisted many tasks. He has little frustration tolerance, and has an adult stance of disdain for the childlike tasks that are difficult for him. The test questions evoked protest that people treated him as if he didn't know anything. He denied learning problems, saying he only did things that were interesting. I concentrated on instruments requiring my training to administer. Over the following week, at my request Mr. Johnston gave Paul the part of the battery where I felt his relationship with Paul would be more of an asset than my training.

Paul was either unwilling or unable to put much effort into the WISC-R subtests, and finally refused to continue. The scores tell little. Paul's general understanding of life situations, his reading comprehension, and his sentence structure on the writing sample, suggest normal intelligence.

Reading decoding is adequate for his age and grade. [Note: test standards change over time. Soon after this, a revision of the WRAT with higher standards was published.] Although the overall reading comprehension score is meaningfully below grade level, Paul succeeded on a

(continued)

Paul *(continued)*

paragraph that would have scored a 9th-grade level if he had succeeded on all preceding items. This suggests that attention and concentration may detract from reading success. He said he reads newspaper classified ads for motorcycles. He would not complete the writing sample, but did write one sentence and some dictated phrases requiring capitalization and punctuation. Findings concur with the teacher's impression of a serious deficiency in written expression. Math is also below grade level, but there is no problem with math concepts, and there are probably other students in the class at the same level. Motivation and application would be a greater problem than computational skills.

In the interview, he refused to discuss the early traumatic events of his life, but was willing to talk about his present family and situation. We fell into talking in the veiled language of adults discussing sensitive matters in front of a child, which may have been his only model for family discussion. Encouraging him to talk about a topic taboo at home started him thinking. At first he said he wanted to remain with his aunt. Later he expressed mixed feelings. The Sentence Completions he told Mr. Johnston later in the week openly expressed many feelings, including that his place is with his adult brothers in another state, and he wants to go there.

Paul's drawings showed a fragmentation of the self reminiscent of the family break-up. Drawings and Sentence Completions both tell that Paul longs for and needs a male figure at home. Sentence Completions content also includes anger over school frustration, and desire to by-pass childhood and be an instant adult.

Follow-up:

Two days after Mr. Johnston finished administering the achievements and Sentence Completions, Paul escalated his school misbehavior to the point that he was asked to leave the school. It was suggested to his aunt that he leave her home as well and return to his brothers. I believe the examination helped Paul express and sort out his feelings. Although he did not plan his outburst, it brought about his desired goal.

After the outburst, he called his teacher at home to apologize and thank everyone for helping him, including this examiner.

Summary:

This examination did not yield enough test scores needed for identification of an educational handicap. It suggests that Paul is a

(continued)

Paul *(continued)*

learning-disabled boy of normal intelligence, with difficulties in attention, concentration, and written expression. He was brutalized by early traumatic experiences and, besides whatever impulsivity he may originally have had, has since lacked the external controls necessary for learning self-control, and does not accept adult authority. Without intervention, he is in danger of becoming delinquent.

His relationship with his aunt was doubly ambivalent. She wanted to raise him and have his company and help, but knew she could not provide needed controls. He felt obligated to stay with her until the end, but did not want to be present at the death of another person he loved, a death he may have felt his behavior was hastening.

Recommendations:

1. Extra help and modified assignments in written expression.
2. Review of math operations in the regular classroom.
3. A behavior program for attention and concentration, and verbal respect toward teachers.
4. Consider an evaluation for attention deficit.
5. Paul should have contact with peers who are good role models.
6. Leisure-time activities should be carefully supervised.
7. I would be happy to talk to the staff of his new school on the phone.

Test reports do not contain specific information that might be prejudicial toward students or consultees. The real events alluded to under *Follow-up* are these: Paul swore at Mr. Johnston in front of the class. When asked to apologize, he did it again. Mr. Johnston took him to Denise.

Private schools do not share public schools' anxieties about due process and lawsuits. In addition, Valley Academy represented religious authority to Paul's aunt. When Denise went to her house and told her what to do, she obeyed.

By administrative standards, this examination was a failure. Not enough tests were completed to fulfill requirements for identifying an educational handicap. Some of the tests were administered by an uncertified person. By the time the report was typed, Paul had left the community. The school never received a request for records. Paul hated school, and one of his brothers owned a construction company. It seems likely that he did not enroll in another school, or become identified as a handicapped learner, or complete high school.

But there is life beyond bureaucracy. Conclusions can be drawn from numerically incomplete information. Paul cooperated on some parts of the examination. The information he gave, the parts he completed, and the parts that aroused greater defensiveness permit some conclusions.

When testing was not as widespread as today, consultees often saw the test itself as a magic wand, a naive view examiners tried to discourage. In this case, the test does seem to have been a factor in the outcome.

When he entered adolescence, Paul began to rebel more against controls at home and at school. The referral for testing followed. The examination made him feel that others were attending to his plight, and made him focus on his situation for over a week. When he responded in the only way he could to bring about a change, his interconnected school and family system immediately followed with their own response.

One bit of informal knowledge (see Chapter 4, pp. 106-107) is that small towns with few human services often have a wealth of traditional mutual help networks[1] that enable those services to be extraordinarily effective.

Although it is usually naive at best and self-serving at worst to believe that a troublesome student is necessarily helped by moving out of the district, Paul appeared to have a more appropriate family structure waiting for him than the one he left.

There are many therapeutic influences in people's lives that are not labeled *therapy*. Conventional therapy is one way to influence lives for the better. The conventional situation puts the therapist more in ownership and control, but not all who need help can take advantage of it. Networks extend in many directions, and a contribution to these is still a piece of the action.

You Are Not Required . . .

You are not required to complete the work, but neither are you free to desist from it.

—Rabbi Tarphon

Where Go the Boats?

Dark brown is the river,
  Golden is the sand,
It flows along forever,
  With trees on either hand.

Green leaves a-floating,
  Castles of the foam,
Boats of mine a-boating—
  Where will all come home?

On goes the river
  And out past the mill,
Away down the valley,
  Away down the hill.

Away down the river,
  A hundred miles or more,
Other little children
  Shall bring my boats ashore.

                —Robert Louis Stevenson

APPENDIX 2

Shadows and Reality:
Plato's Allegory of the Cave

And now, I said, let me show in a figure how far our nature is enlightened or unenlightened: — Behold! human beings living in an under-
ground den, which has a mouth open towards the light and reaching

all along the den; here they have been from their childhood, and have their legs and necks chained so that they cannot move, and can only see before them, being prevented by the chains from turning round their heads. Above and behind them a fire is blazing at a distance, and between the fire and the prisoners there is a raised way; and you will see, if you look, a low wall built along the way, like the screen which marionette players have in front of them, over which they show the puppets.

I see.

And do you see, I said, men passing along the wall carrying all sorts of vessels, and statues and figures of animals made of wood and stone and various materials, which appear over the wall? Some of them are talking, others silent.

You have shown me a strange image, and they are strange prisoners.

Like ourselves, I replied; and they see only their own shadows, or the shadows of one another, which the fire throws on the opposite wall of the cave?

True, he said; how could they see anything but the shadows if they were never allowed to move their heads?

And of the objects which are being carried in like manner they would only see the shadows?

Yes, he said.

And if they were able to converse with one another, would they not suppose that they were naming what was actually before them?

Very true.

And suppose further that the prison had an echo which came from the other side, would they not be sure to fancy when one of the passers-by spoke that the voice which they heard came from the passing shadow?

No question, he replied.

To them, I said, the truth would be literally nothing but the shadows of the images.

That is certain.

And now look again, and see what will naturally follow if the prisoners are released and disabused of their error. At first, when any of them is liberated and compelled suddenly to stand up and turn his neck round and walk and look towards the light, he will suffer sharp pains; the glare will distress him, and he will be unable to see the realities of which in his former state he had seen the shadows; and then conceive some one saying to him, that what he saw before was an illusion, but that now, when he is approaching nearer to being and

his eye is turned towards more real existence, he has a clearer vision, —
what will be his reply? And you may further imagine that his instructor is pointing to the objects as they pass and requiring him to name
them, — will he not be perplexed? Will he not fancy that the shadows
which he formerly saw are truer than the objects which are now shown
to him?

Far truer.

REFERENCES

American Psychiatric Association. (1980). *Diagnostic and statistical manual of mental disorders* (3rd ed.). Washington, DC: Author.

American Psychiatric Association. (1987). *Diagnostic and statistical manual of mental disorders* (3rd ed., rev.). Washington, DC: Author.

Aristotle. (1941). Physics. In R. McKeon (Ed.), *The basic works of Aristotle* (pp. 218-394). New York: Random House. (Original work published about 335-323 B.C.)

Austin, J. L. (1961). *Philosophical papers.* Oxford: Clarendon Press.

Bannatyne, A. (1971). *Language, reading, and learning disabilities.* Springfield, IL: Charles C. Thomas.

Barnes, J. A. (1972). *Social networks.* An Addison-Wesley Module in Anthropology (Module 26, pp. 1-29). Reading, MA: Addison-Wesley.

Binet, A., & Simon, T. (1980). *The development of intelligence in children.* Nashville, TN: Williams. (Original work published 1916)

Block, P. (1981). *Flawless consulting.* Austin, TX: Learning Concepts.

Browne, M. W. (1988, February 16). Simple tests developed to diagnose dyslexia. *The New York Times,* p. C5.

Caplan, G. (1970). *The theory and practice of mental health consultation.* New York: Basic Books.

Caplan, G. (1974). *Support systems and community mental health.* New York: Behavioral Publications.

Cohen, J. (1952). A factor-analytically based rationale for the Wechsler-Bellevue. *Journal of Consulting Psychology, 16,* 272-277.

Cohen, J. (1957). The factorial structure of the WAIS between early adulthood and old age. *Journal of Consulting Psychology, 21,* 283-290.

Cohen, J. (1959). The factorial structure of the WISC at ages 7-6, 10-6, and 13-6. *Journal of Consulting Psychology, 23,* 285-299.

Cohen, M. R., & Nagel, E. (1934). *An introduction to logic and scientific method.* New York: Harcourt Brace.

Columbia Associates in Philosophy. (1923). *An introduction to reflective thinking.* Boston: Houghton Mifflin.

Copleston, F. (1961). *A history of philosophy: Vol. 4. Descartes to Leibniz.* Westminster, MD: Newman.

Dumont/Faro WISC-R computer template. (1989). Hudson, NH: Author.

Dumont/Faro WISC-R computer template. (1990). Hudson, NH: Author.

Elkind, D. (1988). *The hurried child.* Reading, MA: Addison-Wesley. (Original work published 1981)

Fearnside, W. W. (1980). *About thinking.* Englewood Cliffs, NJ: Prentice-Hall.

Feigl, H. (1958). The "mental" and the "physical." In H. Feigl, M. Scriven, & G. Maxwell (Eds.), *Minnesota studies in the philosophy of science: Vol. 2. Concepts, theories, and the mind-body problem* (pp. 370-497). Minneapolis: University of Minnesota.

Feuerstein, R., Rand, Y., Hoffman, M. B., & Miller, R. (1980). *Instrumental enrichment.* Baltimore: University Park Press.

Gesell, A., & Ilg, F. L. (1946). *The child from five to ten.* New York: Harper & Row.

Gleick, J. (1984, November 19). Breakthrough in problem solving. *The New York Times,* pp. 1, 19.

Goh, D. S., Teslow, C. J., & Fuller, G. B. (1981). The practice of psychological assessment among school psychologists. *Professional Psychology, 12,* 696-706.

Grossman, H. J. (Ed.). (1977). *Manual on terminology and classification in mental retardation.* Washington, DC: American Association on Mental Deficiency.

Hall, C. S., & Lindzey, G. (1970). *Theories of personality* (2nd ed.). New York: Wiley. (Original work published 1957)

Ilg, F. L., & Ames, L. B. (1972). *School readiness: Behavior tests used at the Gesell Institute* (new ed.). New York: Harper & Row. (Original work published 1964)

Interagency Committee on Learning Disabilities. (1987). *Learning disabilities: A report to the U.S. Congress.* Washington, DC: Department of Health and Human Services.

Johnson, D. M. (1955). *The psychology of thought and judgment.* New York: Harper.

Kaufman, A. S. (1976). Verbal-Performance IQ discrepancies on the WISC-R. *Journal of Consulting and Clinical Psychology, 44,* 739-744.

Kaufman, A. S. (1979). *Intelligent testing with the WISC-R.* New York: Wiley.

Kaufman, A. S. (1990). *Assessing adolescent and adult intelligence.* Boston: Allyn & Bacon.

Kaufman, A. S., & Kaufman, N. L. (1983a). *Administration and scoring manual for the Kaufman Assessment Battery for Children.* Circle Pines, MN: American Guidance Service.

Kaufman, A. S., & Kaufman, N. L. (1983b). *Interpretive manual for the Kaufman Assessment Battery for Children.* Circle Pines, MN: American Guidance Service.

Kuhn, T. S. (1962). *The structure of scientific revolutions.* Chicago: University of Chicago Press.

Lambert, N. M. (1981). Psychological evidence in Larry P. v. Wilson Riles: An evaluation by a witness for the defense. *American Psychologist, 36,* 937-952.

Lansing School District. (1989). *Learning disabilities guidelines: The identification of students with specific learning disabilities.* Lansing, MI: Author.

Lee, H. N. (1947). Metaphysics as hypothesis. *Journal of Philosophy, 44,* 344-351.

MacNeice, L. (1949). *Collected poems 1925-1948.* London: Faber & Faber.

Maier, P. (1989, July 31). The dissertation that would not die. *The New York Times Book Review,* pp. 11-12.

Mannheim, K. (1968). The sociology of knowledge. In *Ideology and utopia* (pp. 237-280). New York: Harcourt Brace. (Original work published 1936)

Maslow, A. H. (1987). *Motivation and personality* (3rd ed.). New York: Harper & Row. (Original work published 1954)

Meehl, P. E. (1954). *Clinical versus statistical prediction.* Minneapolis: University of Minnesota Press.

Meehl, P. E. (1958). When shall we use our heads instead of the formula? In H. Feigl, M. Scriven, & G. Maxwell (Eds.), *Minnesota studies in the philosophy of science: Vol. 2. Concepts, theories, and the mind-body problem* (pp. 498-506). Minneapolis: University of Minnesota Press.

Meehl, P. E. (1973). Why I do not attend case conferences. In *Psychodiagnosis: Selected papers* (pp. 225-302). Minneapolis: University of Minnesota Press.

Minnesota Department of Education. (1990). *Draft criteria for specific learning disabilities.* St. Paul: Author.

Mitchell, R. E., & Trickett, E. J. (1980). Task force report: Social networks as mediators of social support. *Community Mental Health Journal, 16,* 27-44.

Moore, D. S., & McCabe, G. P. (1989). *Introduction to the practice of statistics.* New York: Freeman.

Murphy, L. B. (1973). The stranglehold of norms on the individual child. *Childhood Education, 49,* 343-349.

National Association of School Psychologists. (1986). *Position statement on rights without labels.* Washington, DC: Author.

New Hampshire Department of Education. (1988). *New Hampshire standards for the education of handicapped students.* Concord, NH: Author.

Orton, S. T. (1925). "Word-blindness" in school children. *Archives of Neurology and Psychiatry, 14,* 581-615.

Perspectives. (1987, June). *The School Psychologist,* pp. 1, 3-5.

Pines, M. (1975, December). In praise of "invulnerables." *APA Monitor,* p. 7.

Pirsig, R. M. (1974). *Zen and the art of motorcycle maintenance.* New York: Morrow.

Plato. (1892). Meno. In B. Jowett (Trans.), *The dialogues of Plato* (3rd ed., Vol. 1, pp. 249-380). Oxford: Oxford University Press. (Original work published about 370 B.C.)

Plato. (1892). The Republic. In B. Jowett (Trans.), *The dialogues of Plato* (3rd ed., Vol. 2, pp. 1-499). Oxford: Oxford University Press. (Original work published about 370 B.C.)

Poetry award winner. (1990, October). *Communique,* p. 16.

Russell, B. (1940). *An inquiry into meaning and truth.* London: Allen & Unwin.

Sarbin, T. R. (1986). Prediction and clinical inference: Forty years later. *Journal of Personality Assessment, 50,* 362-369.

Sattler, J. M. (1982). *Assessment of children's intelligence and special abilities* (2nd ed.). Boston: Allyn & Bacon.

Sattler, J. M. (1988). *Assessment of children* (3rd ed.). San Diego: Author.

Seligman, M. E. P. (1975). *Helplessness.* San Francisco: W. H. Freeman.

Silverstein, A. B. (1982). Pattern analysis as simultaneous statistical inference. *Journal of Consulting and Clinical Psychology, 50,* 234-240.

Stanovich, K. E. (1986). Cognitive processes and the reading problems of learning-disabled children: Evaluating the assumption of specificity. In J. K. Torgeson & B. Y. Z. Wong (Eds.), *Psychological and educational perspectives on learning disabilities* (pp. 87-131). Orlando, FL: Academic Press.

Stevenson, R. L. (1923). *A child's garden of verses.* Chicago: Whitman. (Original work published 1885)

Tarphon [Rabbi]. *Pirke Abot.* Cited in A. B. Giamatti, Baccalaureate address, May, 1984, Yale University, New Haven, CT. (Original work published 2nd century of the Common Era)

Taylor, R. (1990, March). So human a machine. *University of Minnesota Update*, pp. 5-7.

Telzrow, C. F., & Williams, J. L. (1982). *LD discrepancy formula: A handbook*. Maple Heights, OH: Cuyahoga Special Education Service Center.

Thompson, D. W. (1961). *On growth and form*. Cambridge: Cambridge University Press. (Original work published 1917)

Thorndike, E. L. (1922). Measurement in education. In *Twenty-first yearbook of the National Society for the Study of Education: Intelligence tests and their use* (pp. 1-9). Bloomington, IL: Public School Publishing Company.

Thorndike, R. M., Hagen, E. P., & Sattler, J. M. (1986). *Technical manual for the Stanford-Binet Intelligence Scale: Fourth edition*. Chicago: Riverside.

Vitruvius [Pollio, Vitruvius]. (1960). *The ten books on architecture* (M. H. Morgan, Trans.). New York: Dover. (Original work published ca. 27 B.C.)

Wallace, G., & McLoughlin, J. A. (1975). *Learning disabilities: Concepts and characteristics*. Columbus: Charles E. Merrill.

Wallas, G. (1926). *The art of thought*. New York: Harcourt Brace.

Wertheimer, M. (1959). *Productive thinking* (enlarged ed.). New York: Harper. (Original work published 1945)

Whelan, T., & Carlson, C. (1986). Books in school psychology: 1970 to the present. *Professional School Psychology, 1*, 279-289.

Willis, J. O. (1990). *Guide to identification of learning disabilities*. Concord, NH: New Hampshire State Department of Education, Bureau for Special Education Services.

NOTES

This book was developed from a presentation for the Eleventh Northern New England Educational Tests, Measurements, and Evaluation Conference on March 29, 1989, at Plymouth State College, Plymouth, NH.

INTRODUCTION

[1]The original of this often but not exactly quoted statement is, "Whatever exists, exists in some amount. To measure it is simply to know its varying amounts" (E. L. Thorndike, 1922, p. 9).

[2]The original quotation, as best can be remembered, is, "If what I am teaching can be measured, then I am teaching the wrong things." Robert E. O'Neill, who has used this statement to exemplify the anti-empiricist viewpoint, remembers reading it in the mid 1960s. He believes it was by a professor at Columbia University, but does not recall the exact source.

[3]This figure of speech is from Block (1981, p. 20).

[4]One of the reasons school examiners have so many political problems, discussed in Chapter 6, pp. 181-184, is a professional identity problem. There is no profession that represents the school examiner. The recommendations to profession leaders are directed to special education and psychology, respectively.

CHAPTER 1

[1]This book tells many of my own practices. This is not intended as a general recommendation of these practices. I believe that such choices as reporting

style and test usage are highly specific to individual situations, and practitioners should be left to their choice.

Since writing the reports in this book, I have stopped reporting percentile ranks because so many teachers confuse them with percentage grades. They will say something like, "He did really badly on the California Achievement Tests. He was only in the 37th percentile." When I point out that this rank is in the average range and corresponds to an IQ of 95, they look surprised, and probably promptly forget information so dissonant with their belief.

[2]The rule for the V–P discrepancy is also given by Sattler (1982, p. 195; 1988, p. 167).

CHAPTER 2

[1]I once asked, "How do you say, 'The [parent] is extremely stupid?' " Wilhelmina Franklin answered, "[Parent] is a very limited person."

[2]Apologies to Michael Kluznik ("Poetry award winner," 1990). Whether or not he has yet written a novel, he is both a school psychologist *and* a good writer.

[3]Linda Walbridge was Acting Head of the Psychology Department of Laconia State School, Laconia, NH (now Laconia Developmental Services).

[4]Gordon C. G. Thomas, Laconia, NH.

[5]For this perception, I am indebted to Jeffrey Page, School Psychologist, Henniker School District, Henniker, NH.

CHAPTER 3

[1]Achievements are included with ability tests in some batteries, most notably the Kaufman Assessment Battery for Children and the Woodcock-Johnson Psycho-Educational Battery.

[2]Whether to give tests requiring motor skills to children with motor handicaps depends on whether there is greater need to obtain the highest possible IQ score, or highlight weaknesses.

CHAPTER 4

[1]The words *data* and *information* are used here interchangeably. Before the advent of *information* processing, *data* referred specifically to observed and recorded facts, especially numbers, whereas *information* was used more broadly to mean any knowledge, especially verbal, whether observed or acquired some other way. Information processing has made the terms equivalent, but some of the old baggage remains.

[2]The syllogism has been replaced on the contemporary scene by the logical calculus, which includes the syllogism and far more, but suffers the same limitations discussed here as the syllogism.

[3]For those aware of the historical conflict, this discussion assumes existential import.

[4]This estimate is attributed to Anneliese Pontius, Harvard Medical School, by Browne (1988).

[5]For a discussion of the prevalence of learning disabilities, see Wallace and McLaughlin (1975).

[6]The probability was calculated as follows:

Given: 2/3 of LD persons have $P > V$; 1/6 of the population has $P > V$; 1/10 of the population are LD.

Those who are LD and have $P > V = 1/10 \times 2/3 = 1/15$ of the population.

Those who are *not* LD and have $P > V = 1/6 - 1/15 = 1/10$ of the population.

Those who have $P > V$ and are LD $= 1/15$ of the population.

Those who have $P > V$ and are *not* LD $= 1/6 - 1/15 = 1/10$ of the population.

Therefore, among those who have $P > V$,

the ratio of LD to *not* LD is $1/15 : 1/10 = 2 : 3$, or 2 out of 5, or 40%.

[7]Max Wertheimer (1945/1959) calls this the *inner relation* in the mathematical and spatial problems he presents.

[8]Meehl (1958, p. 503) cites Carnap and the British school as including logical evidence in probability.

[9]The discussion of cause appears in Aristotle's (ca. 335-323 B.C./1941, pp. 240-241) *Physics,* Book II, Chapter C, 3.

[10]This homely and practical bit of reasoning is actually equivalent to Pascal's proof of the existence of God. (See Copleston, 1961, pp. 169-171.)

[11]In the *Meno* (Plato, ca. 385 B.C./1892).

[12]The 95% level of *confidence* means exactly the same thing as the 5% level of *significance* cited in Kaufman's practitioners' rules, p. 9, but the emphasis is on the doughnut instead of the hole, so to speak. It represents a 95% probability that each score will fall *within* the band of error designated. If a score falls outside that band of error, it is assumed to show a real difference. The other side of the coin is a 5% probability that each score will fall *outside* the band of error by chance, when there is no real difference (the "null hypothesis"). This usage follows the Kaufman Assessment Battery for Children (Kaufman & Kaufman, 1983a, p. 58). To make matters more confusing, the terms *level of confidence* and *level of significance* are used interchangeably. The Stanford-Binet: 4th edition (Thorndike, Hagen, & Sattler, 1986, p. 132) uses the 5% figure instead of the 95% figure for "level of confidence."

[13]The main idea for this paragraph was contributed by Lynda Boyd, Coordinator of Speech Services, Laconia School District, Laconia, NH.

[14]See Wertheimer (1945/1959, p. 121).

[15]I have specified this program because it is the only one that showed significant differences. *Dumont/Faro* (1989, 1990) is produced privately and distributed chiefly locally.

Although many consumers of computerized programs use them for mechanical interpretation, the *Dumont/Faro* (1989, 1990) manual explicitly states that it is intended as a source of hypotheses, not blind final diagnosis.

CHAPTER 5

[1]See Kaufman, 1979, pp. 70-99.

[2]Dorcus Maskell, Abenaki Self-Help Association, Swanton, VT, was very helpful in providing this information. I also asked her for a suitable name for this child. Maskell asked an older woman in the group, who suggested Running Water. I translated this to Brook, in keeping with her present suburban surroundings; but omitted the usual final *e* as not consistent with native American values.

CHAPTER 6

[1]See, for example, the recommendations of the Interagency Committee on Learning Disabilities, 1987, pp. 219-222.

[2]The penalty for politically wrong opinions in graduate school is illustrated by the story of Frank Bourgin, the acceptance of whose dissertation was delayed 46 years (Maier, 1989). The novel *Zen and the Art of Motorcycle Maintenance* (Pirsig, 1974), also features graduate school political problems.

APPENDIX 1

[1]For background material on networks, see Barnes (1972), Caplan (1974), and Mitchell and Trickett (1980).

AUTHOR INDEX

SUBJECT INDEX

Printed in the United States
18056LVS00007B/58